On Democracy

e.b.
white

on
democracy

with an introduction by Jon Meacham

edited by Martha White

HARPER

An Imprint of HarperCollins*Publishers*

FIRST EDITION

Designed by Fritz Metsch

Library of Congress Cataloging-in-Publication Data

White, E. B. (Elwyn Brooks), author. | White, Martha, editor.
On democracy / E. B. White; edited by Martha White; foreword by Jon
Meacham.
p. cm.
ISBN 978-0-06-290543-7
1. United States—Civilization—20th century. 2. National characteris-
tics, American. 3. Democracy—United States. I. Literary collections—
Essays.   II.   Political   science—political   ideologies—Democracy.
III. History—United States—20th century.
E169.1.W45   2019
973'.9—dc23   2018045976

19 20 21 22 23 LSC   10 9 8 7 6 5 4 3 2 1

An hour of freedom is worth a barrel of slops.

—*Charlotte's Web*

A law has to be fair to everybody.

—*Stuart Little*

Safety is all well and good: I prefer freedom.

—*The Trumpet of the Swan*

Contents

Introduction

> To hold America in one's thoughts is like holding a
> love letter in one's hand—it has so special a meaning.
>
> —E. B. WHITE

Franklin D. Roosevelt couldn't get enough of the piece. At the suggestion of his advisor Harry Hopkins, the New Dealer turned wartime consigliere, the president of the United States took a moment away from the pressures of global war to read a July 3, 1943, "Notes and Comment" essay from *The New Yorker*. Occasioned by a letter from the Writers' War Board, a group of authors devoted to shaping public opinion about the Allied effort in World War II—the board was led by the mystery novelist Rex Stout, the creator of Nero Wolfe, the orchid-loving New York City detective—the small item tackled the largest of subjects. Speaking in the magazine's omniscient vernacular, the *New Yorker* author wrote, "We received a letter from the Writers' War Board the other day asking for a statement on 'The Meaning of Democracy,'" continuing:

> Surely the Board knows what democracy is. It is the line that forms on the right. It is the don't in don't shove. It is the hole in the stuffed shirt

through which the sawdust slowly trickles; it is the dent in the high hat. Democracy is the recurrent suspicion that more than half of the people are right more than half of the time. It is the feeling of privacy in the voting booths, the feeling of communion in the libraries, the feeling of vitality everywhere. Democracy is a letter to the editor. Democracy is the score at the beginning of the ninth. It is an idea which hasn't been disproved yet, a song the words of which have not gone bad. It's the mustard on the hot dog and the cream in rationed coffee.

FDR thought it brilliant. "I LOVE IT!" he said, "with a sort of rising inflection on the word 'love,'" according to the Hopkins biographer and playwright Robert E. Sherwood. The president read the piece to different gatherings, punctuating his recitation with a homey coda (or at least as homey as the squire of Hyde Park ever got): "Them's my sentiments exactly."

They were, importantly, the sentiments of the author of the "Notes and Comment," the longtime *New Yorker* contributor E. B. White, whose writings on freedom and democracy, collected here by his granddaughter Martha White, captivate us still, all these years distant. Few things are as perishable as prose written for magazines (sermons come close, as do the great majority of political speeches), but White, arguably the finest occasional essayist of the twentieth century, endures because he wrote plainly and honestly about the things that matter the most, from life on his farm in Maine to the lives of nations and of peoples. Known popularly more for his books for children (*Charlotte's Web* and *Stuart Little*) than for his corpus of essays, White is that rarest of figures, a writer whose ordinary run of work is so extraordinary that it repays our attention decades after his death.

Hence the value of the collection you are holding in your hands. White lived and wrote through several of the most contentious hours in our history, ones in which America itself felt at best in the dock and at worst on the scaffold. The Great Depression, World War II, the McCarthyite Red Scare, the Cold War, the civil rights movement—all unfolded under White's watchful eye as he composed pieces for *The New Yorker* and for *Harper's*. He was especially gifted at evoking the universal through the exploration of the particular, which is one of the cardinal tasks of the essayist. His work touched on politics but was not, in the popular sense, political, and the writings here underscore the role of the quiet observer in the great dramas of history. For White was not a charismatic speaker—he avoided the platform all his life—nor was he an activist or even a partisan in the way we think of the terms. He was, rather, a wry but profound voice in the large chorus of American life.

In the first days of World War II, in the lovely American September of 1939, after Nazi Germany launched the invasion of Poland, plunging Europe into a war that would last nearly six years, White described a day spent on the waters in Maine. "It struck me as we worked our way homeward up the rough bay with our catch of lobsters and a fresh breeze in our teeth that this was what the fight was all about," he wrote. "This was it. Either we would continue to have it or we wouldn't, this right to speak our own minds, haul our own traps, mind our own business, and wallow in the wide, wide sea."

That fight seems to be unfolding still in the first decades of the twenty-first century, a time when an opportunistic real estate and reality TV showman from White's beloved New York has risen to the pinnacle of American politics by marshaling and, in some cases, manufacturing fears about changing demography and identity in the life of the Republic. We can't know for certain what White would have made of Trump or of Twitter, but we can safely say that E. B. White's America, the one described in this collection, is a better, fairer, and more congenial place than the forty-fifth president's. Reflecting on the Munich Pact of 1938, the agreement, negotiated by British prime minister Neville Chamberlain, that emboldened Adolf Hitler to press on with his campaign to build a thousand-year Reich, White wrote, "Old England, eating swastika for breakfast instead of kipper, is a sight I had as lief not lived to see. And though I'm no warrior, I would gladly fight for the things which Nazism seeks to destroy." Reading him now, at a time when so many Americans live with sights we would have lief not lived to see, is at once reassuring and challenging, for White's America, which should be *our* America, is worth a glad fight.

Born in Mount Vernon, New York, in 1899, Elwyn Brooks White, the youngest of six children, grew up in comfort. "If an unhappy childhood is indispensable for a writer, I am ill-equipped: I missed out on all that and was neither deprived nor unloved," he recalled. His father was a successful businessman who created a secure enclave for his family in Westchester County, just twenty-five minutes from New York City. "Our big house at 101 Summit Avenue was my castle," E. B. White, who was nicknamed "En," wrote. "From it I emerged to do battle, and into it I retreated when I was frightened or in trouble." There were summers in Maine, public school in Westchester, the warmth of a sprawling family. He was sensitive, too, from an early age. "The normal fears and worries of every child were in me developed to a high degree; every day was an awesome prospect. I was uneasy about practically everything: the uncertainty of the future, the dark of the attic, the panoply and discipline of school, the transitoriness of life, the mystery of the church and of God, the frailty of the body, the sadness of afternoon, the shadow of sex, the distant challenge of love and marriage, the far-off problem of a livelihood. I brooded about them all, lived with them day by day."

White's father, Samuel Tilly White, perhaps sensing

something of his youngest child's anxious nature, wrote the lad a cheerful birthday note in 1911. "All hail! With joy and gladness we salute you on your natal day," the senior White wrote. "May each recurring anniversary bring you earth's best gifts and heaven's choicest blessings. Think today on your mercies. You have been born in the greatest and best land on the face of the globe under the best government known to men. Be thankful then that you are an American. Moreover you are the youngest child of a large family and have profited by the companionship of older brothers and sisters. . . . [W]hen you are fretted by the small things of life remember that on this your birthday you heard a voice telling you to look up and out on the great things of life and beholding them say—surely they all are mine."

From an early age, then, White was exhorted to think of America in the most reverential of ways. For all its faults, the nation was a place of particular merit, and a place worth defending. At eighteen, he debated whether to enlist in the Great War, but decided against it. (He also thought about joining the ambulance corps on the grounds that he "would rather save than destroy men.") Instead, he headed for Cornell University, in Ithaca, New York, and became a writer who did indeed look up and out (as well as inward).

The founding of *The New Yorker* magazine in 1925 proved a turning point for White and for American letters. Brought into being by Harold Ross, the weekly was, like Ross himself, chaotic and brilliant. "The cast of characters in those early days," White recalled, "was as shifty as the characters in a floating poker game." James Thurber was among them, as was Katharine Angell, who became Mrs. White in 1929. "During the day I saw her in operation at the office," White recalled. "At the end of the day, I watched her bring the whole mess home with her in a cheap and bulging portfolio. The light burned late, our bed was lumpy with page proofs, and our home was alive with laughter and the pervasive spirit of her dedication and her industry."

The year he married Katharine, White approvingly cited a dissenting opinion of Supreme Court justice Oliver Wendell Holmes, thus inaugurating, in a sense, the canon of his work on freedom and democracy. Reading reports of a commencement speech at West Point by the secretary of war, White wrote that he hoped the young graduates would heed a recent observation of Holmes's: "All West Point graduates should read [Holmes's] words, brighter than sword-thrusts: '. . . if there is any principle of the Constitution that more imperatively calls for attachment than any other it is the principle of free thought—not free thought for those who agree with us but freedom for the thought we hate.'"

He was not a predictable party man. Musing about fashionable talk of a government-controlled economy in the middle of the Depression, White wrote, "Much as we hope that something can be done to adjust the State, reduce inequalities in fortune, and right wrong, we are yet skeptical about the abandonment of private enterprise. . . . Cooperation and public spirit are, we do not doubt, increasingly necessary in the scheme of our economy; but we wonder how far they go in our blood, and whether great music will be written under the guidance of a central planning board whose duty it shall be to coordinate our several harmonics." And when President Roosevelt proposed to pack the Supreme Court after the 1936 presidential election in order to ensure rulings friendlier to the New Deal, White was having none of it. Americans, White wrote, should "decline to follow a leader, however high-minded, who proposes to take charge of affairs because he thinks he knows all the answers."

In June 1940, as the Germans marched into Paris, White weighed in for *The New Yorker*. "To many Americans, war started (spiritually) years ago with the torment of the Jews," White wrote. "To millions of others, less sensitive to the overtones of history, war became actual only when Paris became German. We looked at the faces in the street today, and war is at last real, and the remaining step is merely the transformation of fear into resolve. . . . Democracy is now asked to mount its honor and decency on wheels, and to manufacture, with all the electric power at its command, a world which can make all people free and perhaps many people contented. We believe and shall continue to believe that even that is within the power of men."

The common denominators in White's thinking

about democracy were a sense of fair play and a love of liberty. He was for that which defended and expanded freedom, and he was against that which did not. "If it is boyish to believe that a human being should live free," he wrote in September 1940, "then I'll gladly arrest my development and let the rest of the world grow up."

And he was quite willing to call the rest of world onto a rhetorical carpet if circumstances warranted it. Chatting with other New Yorkers in the fall of 1940, a time when isolationism remained strong in the United States despite the harrowing fall of France and the Battle of Britain, White was disappointed that one man, "discovering signs of zeal [about the war] creeping into my blood, berated me for having lost my detachment, my pure skeptical point of view. He announced that he wasn't going to be swept away by all this nonsense, but would prefer to remain in the role of innocent bystander, which he said was the duty of any intelligent person."

At least one intelligent person, White, chose to disagree. "The least a man can do at such a time is to declare himself and tell where he stands," he wrote. "I believe in freedom with the same burning delight, the same faith, the same intense abandon which attended its birth on this continent more than a century and a half ago. I am writing my declaration rapidly, much as though I were shaving to catch a train. Events abroad give a man a feeling of being pressed for time. . . . I just want to tell, before I get slowed down, that I am in love with freedom and that it is an affair of long standing and that it is a fine state to be in, and that I am deeply suspicious of people who are beginning to adjust to fascism and dictators merely because they are succeeding in war. From such adaptable natures a smell arises. I pinch my nose."

Freedom was not optional; nor was it, in the first instance, political. Working within an ancient Western tradition that viewed liberty as an inherent right and free will as the oxygen of humanity, White traced freedom to its intuitive origins:

> [Freedom begins] with the haunting intimation (which I presume every child receives) of his mystical inner life; of God in man; of nature publishing herself through the "I." This elusive sensation is moving and memorable. It comes early in life; a boy, we'll say, sitting on the front steps on a summer night, thinking of nothing in particular, suddenly hearing as with a new perception and as though for the first time the pulsing sound of crickets, overwhelmed with the novel sense of identification with the natural company of insects and grass and night, conscious of a faint answering cry to the universal perplexing question: "What is 'I'?" Or a little girl, returning from the grave of a pet bird, leaning with her elbows on the window sill, inhaling the unfamiliar draught of death, suddenly seeing herself as part

of the complete story. Or to an older youth, en-
countering for the first time a great teacher who
by some chance or mood awakens something and
the youth beginning to breathe as an individual
and conscious of strength in his vitals. I think
the sensation must develop in many men as a
feeling of identity with God—an eruption of the
spirit caused by allergies and the sense of divine
existence as distinct from mere animal existence.
This is the beginning of the affair with freedom.

As he often did with such grace and fluidity, White
turned from the intimate to the general:

The United States, almost alone today, offers the
liberties and the privileges and the tools of free-
dom. In this land the citizens are still invited to
write plays and books, to paint their pictures, to
meet for discussion, to dissent as well as to agree,
to mount soapboxes in the public square, to enjoy
education in all subjects without censorship, to
hold court and judge one another, to compose mu-
sic, to talk politics with their neighbors without
wondering whether the secret police are listen-
ing, to exchange ideas as well as goods, to kid the
government when it needs kidding, and to read
real news of real events instead of phony news
manufactured by a paid agent of the state. . . . To
be free, in a planetary sense, is to feel that you

belong to earth. To be free, in a societal sense, is to feel at home in a democratic framework.

White's writings are remarkably free of cant and of cliché, as one might expect from the coauthor of *The Elements of Style*. Bombast bored him, and he loved being let alone. Writing in *Paris Review*, Brendan Gill, a fellow *New Yorker* mainstay, once observed, "Andy White is small and wiry, with an unexpectedly large nose, speckled eyes, and an air of being just about to turn away, not on an errand of any importance but as a means of remaining free to cut and run without the nuisance of prolonged good-byes."

White's patriotism is clear-eyed; his nationalism nonexistent. A case in point: in the aftermath of Pearl Harbor, he wrote warmly of American values, noting, "America has been at a great disadvantage in relation to the Axis. In this country we are used to the queer notion that any sort of sporting contest must be governed by a set of rules. We think that the football can't be kicked off until after the whistle is blown. We believe the prize fighter can't be socked until he has come out of his corner. . . . So it was quite to be expected that America grew purple and pink with rage and fury when the Japanese struck us without warning."

And yet White simultaneously believed, and began to argue in the first week of December 1941, that the future belonged to the supranationalists—those who saw that national rivalries were perennial and fatal and had to give way to a broader system of global governance.

"The passionate love of Americans for their America will have a lot to do with winning the war," White wrote. "It is an odd thing though: the very patriotism on which we now rely is the thing that must eventually be in part relinquished if the world is ever to find a lasting peace and an end to these butcheries." Musing on the snow swirling outside his window in these final weeks of the year, White went on: "Already you can see the beginnings of the big post-war poker game, for trade, for air routes and airfields, for insular possessions, and for all the rest of it," he wrote Harold Ross in the fall of 1944. "I hate to see millions of kids getting their guts blown out because all these things are made the prizes of nationality. Science is universal, music is universal, sex is universal, chow is universal, and by God government better be, too."

He would make the case, unsuccessfully, for years, most explicitly in a 1946 book entitled *The Wild Flag*. Whatever White's (self-acknowledged) weaknesses as an architect of a kind of technocratic New Jerusalem, he remained an astute critic of democracy's rivals. In a piece on fascism, he defined the phenomenon as "a nation founded on bloodlines, political expansion by surprise and war, murder or detention of unbelievers, transcendence of state over individual, obedience to one leader, contempt for parliamentary forms, plus some miscellaneous gymnastics for the young and a general feeling of elation. . . . Fascism is openly against people-in-general, in favor of people-in-particular."

After World War II, he worried about fascistic tendencies in America, the very nation that had done so much to defeat the Axis. In 1947 he spoke out against the New York *Herald Tribune*'s editorial support for blacklisting those who did not swear loyalty to the United States. The anticommunist campaign, White wrote in a letter to the editor of the paper, meant that employees had to "be required to state their beliefs in order to hold their jobs. The idea is inconsistent with our Constitutional theory and has been stubbornly opposed by watchful men since the early days of the Republic. . . . I hold that it would be improper for any committee or any employer to examine my conscience. They wouldn't know how to get into it, they wouldn't know what to do when they got in there, and I wouldn't let them in anyway. Like other Americans, my acts and my words are open to inspection—not my thoughts or my political affiliation."

His work touched on the central domestic struggle of the twentieth century, too: the long battle against Jim Crow, the system of racial segregation that had grown out of the failures of Reconstruction in the wake of the Civil War. "The South," he wrote in *The New Yorker* in 1956, "is the land of the sustained sibilant. Everywhere, for the appreciative visitor, the letter S insinuates itself into the scene: the sound of sea and sand, in the singing shell, in the heat of sun and sky, in the sultriness of the gentle hours, in the siesta, in the stir of birds and insects." But, White added, "In contrast to the softness of its music, the South is also hard and cruel and prickly."

He was reporting about a visit to Jim Crow Florida, calling himself "a beachcomber from the North, which is my present status." It had been two years since the U.S. Supreme Court had struck down school segregation, and not long before, a collection of legislators from the Old Confederacy had issued a defiant Southern Manifesto pledging to defy federal efforts to integrate the region. Writing from Florida, White described a conversation with his cook, a Finnish woman, about "the mysteries of bus travel in the American Southland." "When you get on the bus," White told her, "I think you'd better sit in one of the front seats—the seats in the back are for colored people."

The cook, who was white, saw through it all. "A look of great weariness came into her face, as it does when we use too many dishes, and she replied, 'Oh, I know—isn't it silly!'"

Then came a brief meditation by White that captured much about what W. E. B. Du Bois had called "the problem of the color-line":

Her remark, coming as it did all the way from Finland and landing on this sandbar with a plunk, impressed me. The Supreme Court said nothing about silliness, but I suspect it may play more of a role than one might suppose. People are, if anything, more touchy about being thought silly than they are about being thought unjust. I note that one of the arguments in the recent manifesto of Southern congressmen in support of the doctrine of "separate but equal" was that it had been founded on "common sense." The sense that is common to one generation is uncommon to the next. Probably the first slave ship, with Negroes lying in chains on its decks, seemed commonsensical to the owners who operated it and to the planters who patronized it. But such a vessel would not be in the realm of common sense today.

The pressures of the Cold War gave White plenty of opportunities to offer thoughts on democracy, and he took many of them. When universities were debating loyalty and "Americanism," White wrote, "A healthy university in a healthy democracy is a free society, in miniature. The pesky nature of democratic life is that it has no comfortable rigidity; it always hangs by a thread, never quite submits to consolidation or solidification, is always being challenged, always being defended."

The key thing—and White worried about this, volunteering his pen in the cause—is the nature and the fate of the defense in the face of those inevitable challenges. White anticipated the antidemocratic forces of our own era: political tribalism ("We doubt that there

ever was a time in this country when so many peo-
ple were trying to discredit so many other people," he
wrote—in 1952); media saturation ("This country is on
the verge of getting news-drunk anyway; a democracy
cannot survive merely by being well informed, it must
also be contemplative, and wise," he wrote—in 1954);
and the need for a free and disputatious press ("There
is safety in numbers: the papers expose each other's
follies and peccadillos, correct each other's mistakes,
and cancel out each other's biases" he wrote—in 1976).
He believed strongly, too, in the virtues of a diversity
of ownership in the media, arguing that oligarchical
and monopolistic tendencies in terms of the control of
the means of information were bad for democracy, and
therefore a threat to freedom.

White was always mindful about the mind itself,
which he considered, with its cousins the imagination
and the conscience, the wellspring of all good things.
Amid the debates about the role of religious obser-
vance in the public arena in the twentieth century,
he brilliantly laid out an inspired test for those who
would compel others to share their beliefs. "Democ-
racy, if I understand it at all, is a society in which
the unbeliever feels undisturbed and at home. . . .
I believe that our political leaders should live by
faith and should, by deeds and sometimes by prayer,
demonstrate faith, but I doubt that they should advo-
cate faith, if only because such advocacy renders a few
people uncomfortable. The concern of a democracy is

that no honest man shall feel uncomfortable, I don't care who he is, or how nutty he is."

At heart, White's vision of democracy is about generosity of spirit and a kind of self-interested covenant—the best way to guarantee freedom and fair play for ourselves is to guarantee it for others. In this way, anyone who attempts to subvert the system or abridge another's rights is instantly shown to be a hypocrite whose will to power threatens to hijack an ethos where no one kicks the ball until the whistle is blown, and no one can tell you what to think or whom to worship or what to do. In leaving us this understanding of how we have lived, and how we ought to go on living, White is a kind of conversational Thomas Jefferson, a twentieth-century Benjamin Franklin, an accessible James Madison.

A final thought. In early 1942, White was summoned to Washington for several days of meetings about a wartime project: the production of a pamphlet, authored by several of the nation's finest writers (Max Lerner and Reinhold Niebuhr among them), to expound on President Roosevelt's Four Freedoms. A year earlier, in his January 1941 State of the Union address, FDR had first articulated his vision of a united front against the march of dictatorship. "I suppose that every realist knows that the democratic way of life is at this moment being directly assailed in every part of the world—assailed either by arms, or by secret spreading of poisonous propaganda by those who seek to destroy unity and promote discord in nations that are still at peace," Roosevelt had told the Congress. After laying out a practical program for rearmament and aid to the Allied forces, the president broadened his sights. "In the future days, which we seek to make more secure, we look forward to a world founded upon four essential human freedoms," he said. He enumerated the freedom of speech and of conscience and the freedom from want and from fear. "That is no vision of a distant millennium," he added. "It is a definite basis for a kind of world attainable in our own time and generation. That kind of world is the very antithesis of the so-called new order of tyranny which the dictators seek to create with the crash of a bomb."

Now, with the war upon America in the wake of Pearl Harbor, Archibald MacLeish, the poet and Librarian of Congress, wanted White to take charge of a Four Freedoms publication for wide distribution. The task was to expand on Roosevelt's general themes, a job that White found daunting. In letters to Katharine, he was honest about his trepidation. After a series of conversations, including a lovely pasta-and-wine lunch at MacLeish's Georgetown house, White had what he called "thousands of untranscribed notes—the kind of thing you scribble on your program in a dark theatre— and the burden of collecting these into a document which will suit the President and the Supreme Court justices and Mr. Churchill . . . and which will explain to a great many young men why they are about to get stuck in the stomach." There was enough meandering in the debates about the project that White thought about, but did not mention, an obvious possibility. "Two or three times during the proceedings I was tempted to ask why, if the pamphlet was to be an extension and an interpretation of the President's formula, we shouldn't just go and ask him what he meant." They never did, and neither can we. But this collection gives us perhaps the next best thing: we can ask E. B. White about freedom and democracy, and he can answer.

JON MEACHAM

On Democracy

High Ambiguity

This is a fairly well-balanced nation. While our aerial ambassador has been spreading goodwill in the warm and willing little countries of tropical America, work has been progressing satisfactorily on combat planes for the Army Air Corps. Five pursuit ships are being built, called super-hawks. These are so equipped with oxygen tanks that they will be able to wage war seven miles up, at which distance, it occurs to us, the whole thing may be mistaken for a goodwill flight unless people are exceptionally well informed.

Dissenting Supreme Court Justice

We disagree with Secretary of War Good, who told the West Point graduate that the profession of arms is "the most honorable of all professions." It used to be, but it isn't anymore. One profession that is more noble today than that of soldier is that of Dissenting Justice of the Supreme Court. It's more honorable to be a dissenting justice than a brigadier general—more honorable because more important. Secretary of War Good charged his two hundred and ninety-nine brand-new lieutenants with the nobility of courage, self-sacrifice, and devotion to ideals. But not long ago Justice Holmes, dissenting from the opinion of the Supreme Court denying citizenship to Rosika Schwimmer, charged the people of the nation with another kind of nobility. All West Point graduates should read his words, brighter than sword-thrusts: ". . . if there is any principle of the Constitution that more imperatively calls for attachment than any other it is the principle of free thought—not free thought for those who agree with us but freedom for the thought we hate."

Statement of the Foreign Policy
of One Citizen of the United States

(Name on request)

I have no plan
Involving Japan.

I do not wish to crush
Soviet Rush.

I would give France
My last pair of pants.

Germany, as far as I am concerned,
Can consider the other cheek turned.

My only territorial ambition
Is to go fishin'.

I do not feel
Zeal.

I look at a foreign minister
As unnecessary and sinister.

Almost any diplomat
Should be given his hat.

I do not want my family to come to ruin
On account of what other people are doin'.

My life does not impinge
On any other nation's fringe.

And, to reiterate, I have no plan
Involving Japan.

To attachés, members of diets, envoys, delegates,
correspondents, vice-admirals, advocates, firers of
21-gun-salutes, chargés d'affaires, ministers, drafters
of building programs, legislators, lance corporals—
GREETINGS! Know all present:

My life does not impinge
On any other nation's fringe.

And if your eager, restless brains
Are plotting immediate gains,

Know also that I'll be deeply disappointed if, in the
    general ruction
I meet destruction.

And though the diplomatic corps, the army, and the
    navy may wish to spike me,
There must be a hundred million others like me.

Down with Cake

The pious *Herald Tribune*, I see, was mad as hops
That Communist paraders kept the People from the
  shops,
That social demonstrations of the radicals on May
  Day
Were very hard on Altman's, who was cat'ring to
  Milady.
For how could decent citizens reach Draperies and
  Notions
When masses on the sidewalk were expressing mass
  emotions!
If wry, subversive tendencies the Reds must really air,
Why, let them do their marching, said the *Trib*, in
  Union Square,
Or over on First Avenue, among the cheap bazaars,
But not in front of Best's, you know, where nice folks
  park their cars.
For how could tulle and chiffon be the things we
  spend our dime on
While Scottsboro defenders blocked the doors of
  Franklin Simon!

Our chances of recovery, the *Trib* explained, were
    dead,
If our potential purchasers were jostled by the Red;
And social revolution was a rather trying *dee*-tail
To add to all the troubles of the Man Who Sells At
    Retail.

Controlled Opinion

A good deal of time has to be spent, even in the hot weather, worrying about how the country is going to manage its transition to an economy of abundance. We have been reading a pamphlet which describes a plan for the gradual change from private enterprise for profit to public enterprise for the fun of the thing. This plan, first published in the magazine *Common Sense*, proposes a Cooperative Commonwealth, which anybody may join, to operate concurrently with Private Enterprise, until at length everybody has joined the Coop and privacy has petered out. "A sufficient control of the organs of public opinion shall be imposed to prevent the stirring up of hostile opinion during the period of the emergency," says the pamphlet, cheerfully. We bristle at that! (Hear us while we bristle.) We don't mind changing to a different economy, as to a different shirt, but we will not submit, even for a split second, to controlled opinion. If it is controlled, it isn't opinion. Boy, take another Commonwealth away!

Much as we hope that something can be done to adjust the State, reduce inequalities in fortune, and right wrong, we are yet skeptical about the abandonment of private enterprise. So many enterprises are, in essence, private. A poet's enterprise is so much a private affair that it is almost a secret. Thieves are deep in private undertakings. Inventors, we feel sure, are inspired by the privacy of their conjectures and experiments, going about always with thoughts unmentionable. Cooperation and public spirit are, we do not doubt, increasingly necessary in the scheme of our economy; but we wonder how far they go in our blood, and whether great music will be written under the guidance of a central planning board whose duty it shall be to coordinate our several harmonics. We wonder how Love, which is a private emprise, is faring in Russia, where it has recently been made a compulsory attribute, under pain of punishment.

Freedom of the Air
(and the Right to Silence . . .)

Sayre M. Ramsdell, vice-president of the Philco Radio & Television Corporation, has sent us eight questions with the request that we give our "best thought" to them. We are the greatest question-answerer alive, and hasten to reply, in detail. Q. What consideration shall be given the matter of freedom of the air? A. Every. Q. Shall the broadcasting stations, licensed as private-profit institutions to use a certain monopoly wave-band, have the sole right to determine who is to broadcast and what is to be said on the air? A. Yes. Q. What shall be the criteria to govern so-called radio neutrality on controversial issues, and who shall be the guiding factor in deciding such issues? A. The same criteria that govern so-called neutrality in the home, the Senate, and the press. The head of the radio company shall be the guiding factor, and good luck go with him!

(Incidentally, Mr. Paley did very well, we thought, with the Republican National Committee.) Q. What shall be the relation of the government to this great channel of communication—radio—and to what phases of it? A. The government shall have a little station of its own. Q. What principle shall govern the granting or withholding of licenses to bodies? A. The principle of free (usually hot) air. Q. What shall be the attitude of the government in granting licenses for broadcasting stations to labor, educational, veteran, and other non-profit groups? A. Stained glass. Q. Shall the broadcasting companies be permitted to establish their own criteria in charging for time on the air, granted to them by the government as a monopoly, for which they pay nothing? A. Yes. Q. Shall the editorial judgment of the broadcasting private-profit organizations be the deciding factor in determining what the American people shall be permitted to hear on the air? A. Yes.

And now we will ask a question, and answer it. Q. What is the greatest, and least understood, privilege of every American citizen? A. To turn it off.

Political Beneficiaries

We disagree, in a small particular, with Owen D. Young about free speech and the radio. "Freedom of speech for the man whose voice can be heard a few hundred feet is one thing," he told Rollins College students, "But freedom of speech for the man whose voice may be heard around the world is another." We think they are identical. For although the radio has a million ears (and therefore a million times greater reception of ill-advised sounds), it also has a million times greater power of skepticism, analysis, prejudice, and inattention. The beauty of free speech which is free is that it is self-annihilating, whether in tiny amounts or in great amounts; and the menace of speech which is not free is that it is self-perpetuating, like a cellar full of rats.

Our political views may soon gain some much-needed clarity, after a long period of confusion. We have talked lightly of revolution, have spoken praise and blame of federal benevolence, have scoffed at professional liberty-lovers and carped at Communists in wolf's clothing, but gradually our tattered brain begins to see that only one thing matters—the preservation of a certain germ of the democratic cell that makes life (however difficult, however clumsy or unfair) free in spirit. If democracy is going to save its skin, it had better hustle, before the "pay me" principle of economics destroys it. Freedom of utterance is still ours, and is still yours. We happen not to approve of the things Father Coughlin and Dr. Townsend say, but we feel content in a country that guarantees them the right to say those things to millions of listeners and *us* the privilege of expressing disagreement to a few thousand. The land we will not be able to live in is the land of political beneficiaries—where there will be only one word, and the word won't be God.

Now ... the Judiciary

The President, in his Victory Dinner speech, said the shouting against him had broken forth again, as it did in the early days of the New Deal, "and from substantially the same elements of opposition." This is balderdash. The opposition to his plan to bring the judiciary into line[*] is from people who care not about their property, their profits, and their old Lincoln limousines, but who care about their freedom from authority—which was what started the first big doings in this country and may well start the last. We ourselves applauded Mr. Roosevelt's program four years ago, but we decline to follow a leader, however high-minded, who proposes to take charge of affairs because he thinks he knows all the answers. Mr. Roosevelt is not ambitious personally, but he has turned into an Eagle Scout whose

[*]FDR proposed that "whenever a Judge or Justice of any Federal Court has reached the age of seventy and does not avail himself of the opportunity to retire on a pension, a new member shall be appointed by the President then in office, with the approval, as required by the Constitution, of the Senate of the United States."

passion for doing the country a good turn every day has at last got out of hand. His "Now" remarks were a giveaway—the utterances of a petulant savior. America doesn't need to be saved today; it can wait till tomorrow. Meanwhile, Mister, we'll sleep on it.[*]

[*]FDR proposed "That plan has two chief purposes. By bringing into the judicial system a steady and continuing stream of new and younger blood, I hope, first, to make the administration of all Federal justice speedier and, therefore, less costly; secondly, to bring to the decision of social and economic problems younger men who have had personal experience and contact with modern facts and circumstances under which average men have to live and work. This plan will save our national Constitution from hardening of the judicial arteries."

I Say to You, Cheerio

It pleasures me, at end of day,
To hear Boake Carter's baleful lay,
The lullaby of world decay
   When Boake
   Has spoke.

I like to hear him summon us
With all things ominous:
   Munition makers, plotting gain,
   Asylums bulging with insane,
   Cancers that give no hint of pain,
   Insurgency in northern Spain,
   And rivers swollen with the rain.
      For Boake
      Has spoke,
      And it's no joke.

The tired world is slowly swooning
To Philco's automatic tuning.
   I close my eyes, and through my head
   The legions of despair are led.
   I hear their heavy, ruthless tread,
   And shudder with ethereal dread

At news by Boake interpreted.
    For he is master
    Of disaster.

I like to hear the deep, sharp croaking
Of Boake, when he is really Boaking;
    The sinister Carterial thesis:
    A battleship is blown to pieces,
    A town is stricken with paresis,
    A mad king slays his favorite nieces,
    Men strike, plants close, and all work ceases.
        Millions are restive under the yoke,
        Aren't they, Boake?

Oh, twist the dial at end of day,
And hear the prelude to decay,
The Philcolossal world dismay:
    The market breaks – a Fascist scare,
    Twelve Roman priests are bombed at prayer,
    A hundred G-men raid the . . .

                But I see my time is
                up, and so I say to
                you . . . Cheerio!

Standards of Journalism

The widow of a Milwaukee publisher has bequeathed a million dollars so that newspapermen, on their leaves of absence, can study at Harvard. She hopes that this will elevate the standards of journalism in the United States. We do, too, but we're afraid that her plan has its drawbacks. For one thing, newspapermen, as a class, don't get leaves of absence. They either get fired or they take sick and die. For another thing, she has picked the wrong kind of people to go to Harvard—reporters, editorial writers, special writers. Obviously the people who could use a spell at Harvard are the publishers of papers, not the employees. Go into any newspaper office and you'll find it teeming with Harvard men, most of whom need not another term at Cambridge but a dollar and a half to get their shirts back from the laundry. These employees are, by and large, men of high standards. If the papers of the United States could be turned over, suddenly, to reporters, editorial writers, and special writers, the standards of journalism would skyrocket overnight. It is the publishers who hold back a newspaper, not people like J. Otis Swift, Eleanor Roosevelt, and Westbrook Pegler. Why? Because publishers want to make a lot of money so that their widows can leave a million dollars to send somebody back to Harvard. Hearst went to Harvard, and he couldn't elevate a standard if it was rigged up with pulleys.

Total Moral Resistance

An hour or two ago, the news came that France had capitulated. The march of the vigorous and the audacious people continues, and the sound is closer, now, and easier to hear.

To many Americans, war started (spiritually) many years ago with the torment of the Jews. To millions of others, less sensitive to the overtones of history, war became actual only when Paris became German. We looked at the faces in the street today, and war is at last real, and the remaining step is merely the transformation of fear into resolve.

The feeling, at the pit of every man's stomach, that the fall of France is the end of everything will soon change into the inevitable equivalent human feeling— that perhaps this is the beginning of a lot of things. Not all dreamers are dead, or interned, and not all dreams are of conquest. If one type of fantasy can come true by the sheer working of an iron resolve, it is conceivable that another type can also. Two can play at dreaming.

By far the most challenging and interesting word in the victorious Nazi scheme is the word total. The message has been total, and the goal is total. It is the word which most needs study and clarification, because it undeniably is the key to this day's events. We are of the opinion that something of a total nature is in store for this country, and we don't mean dictatorship or vigor. We mean a total rejection of the threat with which we are faced, and a total moral resistance to it. One thing begins to become clear: military defense, pure defense, is no good today. Or, rather, it is not good enough. It assumes a complete knowledge of the extent and nature of military invasion, and this can never exist and at best is just guesswork. President Roosevelt spoke of equipment which would be equal to the task "of any emergency and every defense." These are brave words, but they are just words. It has been demonstrated that to be prepared, in a military way, for "any" emergency is impossible, because the emergency may easily turn out to be a new one, hitherto undreamed of. The Maginot Line was ready for any emergency.

Whatever the military and diplomatic policy of this country, it should recognize not only the peculiar new significance of total desire and total deeds, but the new possibilities. The machine has made the word total into something which is fearful and mystical and at the same time challenging. Democracy is now asked to mount its honor and decency on wheels, and to manufacture, with all the electric power at its command, a world which can make all people free and perhaps many people contented. We believe and shall continue to believe that even that is within the power of men.

Freedom

I have often noticed on my trips up to the city that people have recut their clothes to follow the fashion. On my last trip, however, it seemed to me that people had remodeled their ideas too—taken in their convictions a little at the waist, shortened the sleeves of their resolve, and fitted themselves out in a new intellectual ensemble copied from a smart design out of the very latest page of history. It seemed to me they had strung along with Paris a little too long.

I confess to a disturbed stomach. I feel sick when I find anyone adjusting his mind to the new tyranny which is succeeding abroad. Because of its fundamental strictures, fascism does not seem to me to admit of any compromise or any rationalization, and I resent the patronizing air of persons who find in my plain belief in freedom a sign of immaturity. If it is boyish to believe that a human being should live free, then I'll gladly arrest my development and let the rest of the world grow up.

I shall report some of the strange remarks I heard in New York. One man told me that he thought perhaps the Nazi ideal was a sounder ideal than our constitutional system "because have you ever noticed what fine alert young faces the young German soldiers have in the newsreel?" He added: "Our American youngsters spend all their time at the movies—they're a mess." That was his summation of the case, his interpretation of the new Europe. Such a remark leaves me pale and shaken. If it represents the peak of our intelligence, then the steady march of despotism will not receive any considerable setback at our shores.

Another man informed me that our democratic notion of popular government was decadent and not worth bothering about—"because England is really rotten and the industrial towns there are a disgrace." That was the only reason he gave for the hopelessness of democracy; and he seemed mightily pleased with himself, as though he were more familiar than most with the anatomy of decadence, and had detected subtler aspects of the situation than were discernible to the rest of us.

Another man assured me that anyone who took *any* kind of government seriously was a gullible fool. You could be sure, he said, that there is nothing but corruption "because of the way Clemenceau acted at Versailles." He said it didn't make any difference really about this war. It was just another war. Having relieved himself of this majestic bit of reasoning, he subsided.

Another individual, discovering signs of zeal creeping into my blood, berated me for having lost my detachment, my pure skeptical point of view. He announced that he wasn't going to be swept away by all this nonsense, but would prefer to remain in the role of innocent bystander, which he said was the duty of any intelligent person. (I noticed, however, that he phoned later to qualify his remark, as though he had lost some of his innocence in the cab on the way home.)

Those are just a few samples of the sort of talk that seemed to be going round—talk which was full of defeatism and disillusion and sometimes of a too studied innocence. Men are not merely annihilating themselves at a great rate these days, but they are telling one another enormous lies, grandiose fibs. Such remarks as I heard are fearfully disturbing in their cumulative effect. They are more destructive than dive bombers and mine fields, for they challenge not merely one's immediate position but one's main defenses. They seemed to me to issue either from persons who could never have really come to grips with freedom so as to understand her, or from renegades. Where I expected to find indignation, I found paralysis, or a sort of dim acquiescence, as in a child who is dully swallowing a distasteful pill. I was advised of the growing anti-Jewish sentiment by a man who seemed to be watching the phenomenon of intolerance not through tears of shame but with a clear intellectual gaze, as through a well-ground lens.

The least a man can do at such a time is to declare himself and tell where he stands. I believe in freedom with the same burning delight, the same faith, the same intense abandon which attended its birth on this continent more than a century and a half ago. I am writing my declaration rapidly, much as though I were shaving to catch a train. Events abroad give a man a feeling of being pressed for time. Actually I do not believe I am pressed for time, and I apologize to the reader for a false impression that may be created. I just want to tell, before I get slowed down, that I am in love with freedom and that it is an affair of long standing and that it is a fine state to be in, and that I am deeply suspicious of people who are beginning to adjust to fascism and dictators merely because they are succeeding in war. From such adaptable natures a smell rises. I pinch my nose.

For as long as I can remember I have had a sense of living somewhat freely in a natural world. I don't mean I enjoyed freedom of action, but my existence seemed to have the quality of freeness. I traveled with secret papers pertaining to a divine conspiracy. Intuitively I've always been aware of the vitally important pact which a man has with himself, to be all things to himself, and to be identified with all things, to stand self-reliant, taking advantage of his haphazard connection with a planet, riding his luck, and following his bent with the tenacity of a hound. My first and greatest love affair was with this thing we call freedom, this lady of infinite allure, this dangerous and beautiful and sublime being who restores and supplies us all.

It began with the haunting intimation (which I presume every child receives) of his mystical inner life; of

God in man; of nature publishing herself through the "I." This elusive sensation is moving and memorable. It comes early in life; a boy, we'll say, sitting on the front steps on a summer night, thinking of nothing in particular, suddenly hearing as with a new perception and as though for the first time the pulsing sound of crickets, overwhelmed with the novel sense of identification with the natural company of insects and grass and night, conscious of a faint answering cry to the universal perplexing question: "What is 'I'?" Or a little girl, returning from the grave of a pet bird leaning with her elbows on the window sill, inhaling the unfamiliar draught of death, suddenly seeing herself as part of the complete story. Or to an older youth, encountering for the first time a great teacher who by some chance word or mood awakens something and the youth beginning to breathe as an individual and conscious of strength in his vitals. I think the sensation must develop in many men as a feeling of identity with God—an eruption of the spirit caused by allergies and the sense of divine existence as distinct from mere animal existence. This is the beginning of the affair with freedom.

But a man's free condition is of two parts: the instinctive freeness he experiences as an animal dweller on a planet, and the practical liberties he enjoys as a privileged member of human society. The latter is, of the two, more generally understood, more widely admired, more violently challenged and discussed. It is the practical and apparent side of freedom. The

United States, almost alone today, offers the liberties and the privileges and the tools of freedom. In this land the citizens are still invited to write plays and books, to paint their pictures, to meet for discussion, to dissent as well as to agree, to mount soapboxes in the public square, to enjoy education in all subjects without censorship, to hold court and judge one another, to compose music, to talk politics with their neighbors without wondering whether the secret police are listening, to exchange ideas as well as goods, to kid the government when it needs kidding, and to read real news of real events instead of phony news manufactured by a paid agent of the state. This is a fact and should give every person pause.

To be free, in a planetary sense, is to feel that you belong to earth. To be free, in a social sense, is to feel at home in a democratic framework. In Adolf Hitler, although he is a freely flowering individual, we do not detect either type of sensibility. From reading his book I gather that his feeling for earth is not a sense of communion but a driving urge to prevail. His feeling for men is not that they co-exist, but that they are capable of being arranged and standardized by a superior intellect—that their existence suggests not a fulfillment of their personalities but a submersion of their personalities in the common racial destiny. His very great absorption in the destiny of the German people somehow loses some of its effect when you discover, from his writings, in what vast contempt he holds all people. "I learned," he wrote, ". . . to gain an insight into the unbelievably primitive opinions and arguments of the people." To him the ordinary man is a primitive, capable only of being used and led. He speaks continually of people as sheep, halfwits, and impudent fools—the same people to whom he promises the ultimate in prizes.

Here in America, where our society is based on belief in the individual, not contempt for him, the free principle of life has a chance of surviving. I believe that it must and will survive. To understand freedom is an accomplishment which all men may acquire who set their minds in that direction; and to love freedom is a tendency which many Americans are born with. To live in the same room with freedom, or in the same hemisphere, is still a profoundly shaking experience for me.

One of the earliest truths (and to him most valuable) that the author of *Mein Kampf* discovered was that it is not the written word, but the spoken word, which in heated moments moves great masses of people to noble or ignoble action. The written word, unlike the spoken word, is something which every person examines privately and judges calmly by his own intellectual standards, not by what the man standing next to him thinks. "I know," wrote Hitler, "that one is able to win people far more by the spoken than by the written word. . . ." Later he adds contemptuously: "For let it be said to all knights of the pen and to all the political dandies, especially of today: the greatest changes in this world have never been brought about by a goose quill! No, the pen has always been reserved to motivate these changes theoretically."

Luckily I am not out to change the world—that's being done for me, and at a great clip. But I know that the free spirit of man is persistent in nature; it recurs, and has never successfully been wiped out, by fire or flood. I set down the above remarks merely (in the words of Mr. Hitler) to motivate that spirit, theoretically. Being myself a knight of the goose quill, I am under no misapprehension about "winning people"; but I am inordinately proud these days of the quill, for it has shown itself, historically, to be the hypodermic that inoculates men and keeps the germ of freedom always in circulation, so that there are individuals in every time in every land who are the carriers, the Typhoid Marys, capable of infecting others by mere contact and example. These persons are feared by every tyrant—who shows his fear by burning the books and destroying the individuals. A writer goes about his task today with the extra satisfaction which comes from knowing that he will be the first to have his head lopped off—even before the political dandies. In my own case this is a double satisfaction, for if freedom were denied me by force of earthly circumstance, I am the same as dead and would infinitely prefer to go into fascism without my head than with it, having no use for it anymore and not wishing to be saddled with so heavy an encumbrance.

Intimations

Yesterday the biggest boy in town tried to enlist in the Navy, but the Navy wouldn't take him. They said he was too tall. He is six feet four and a half inches or about twice the height of a Japanese. Apparently the recruiting officer felt this would give America an unfair advantage.

As I write, this is the third day of the war. That is, for most of us it is. There's one lady I know who has it worked out that we have been at war for some years now. She is an inveterate radio listener, and whenever she hears static she thinks it's the Germans, communicating with their local spies. Life has been a vivid thing to her, and war a reality, for a long while. This latest attack on Pearl Harbor was just an incident. At that I suspect she is nearer right than most of us. It is better to hear messages in static than to hear no messages in anything; think of the people who have listened to the rumbling and crackling of National Socialism for the past six or eight years without detecting any ominous sound!

A light fall of snow in the night, and this morning the fields look like a man's face when he has used too much powder after a shave. A few little apples still cling to one of the old trees—they catch the light and perform a frosted miracle of ornamentation. The sheep move about, restlessly, finding little to satisfy them on a hard earth.

How quickly life's accents shifted on that sudden and unforgettable Sunday—the fateful seventh of December. My wife was getting a hot-water bag for somebody, and somehow she managed to lose the stopper down the toilet, beyond recall. This grotesque little incident seemed to upset her to a disproportionate degree: it was because she felt that, now that the war had begun in earnest, there was no excuse for any clumsiness in home nursing. The loss of the stopper suddenly seemed as severe a blow as the loss of a battleship. Life, which for two years had a rather dreamlike quality, came instantly into sharp focus. The time for losing hot-water bag stoppers was over and gone.

America has been at a great disadvantage in relation to the Axis. In this country we are used to the queer notion that any sort of sporting contest must be governed by a set of rules. We think that the football can't be kicked off until after the whistle is blown. We believe the prize fighter can't be socked until he has come out of his corner. We think the fox hunter must tip his hat to the M.F.H. [masters of foxhounds] before he can gallop off after a fox. In this crazy land of ours a tennis player doesn't serve until his opponent is ready. Ever since trouble began inside Germany, years ago, we have hung tight to our sportsmanship, our code of honor, our book of rules, quite incapable of comprehending any other sort of approach to life. Not all the loud denial by Herr Hitler, not the plain statement in his book that the way to get an advantage was to seize it, not the deeds themselves as the little countries were struck down one by one, made much of a dent in our characters. So it was quite to be expected that America grew purple and pink with rage and fury when the Japanese struck us without warning. There are still, on this third day, people who seem to feel that a universal referee will step in and call a penalty.

The passionate love of Americans for their America will have a lot to do with winning the war. It is an odd thing though: the very patriotism on which we now rely is the thing that must eventually be in part relinquished if the world is ever to find a lasting peace and an end to these butcheries.

To hold America in one's thoughts is like holding a love letter in one's hand—it has so special a meaning. Since I started writing this column snow has begun falling again; I sit in my room watching the re-enactment of this stagy old phenomenon outside the window. For this picture, for this privilege, this cameo of New England with snow falling, I would give everything. Yet all the time I know that this very loyalty, this feeling of being part of a special place, this respect for one's native scene—I know that such emotions have had a big part in the world's wars. Who is there big enough to love the whole planet? We must find such people for the next society.

Although supranationalism often seems hopelessly distant or impractical, there is one rather encouraging sign in the sky. We have, lately, at least one large new group of people to whom the planet *does* come first. I mean scientists. Science, however undiscriminating it has seemed in the bestowal of its gifts, has no disturbing club affiliations. It eschews nationality. It is preoccupied with an atom, not an atoll.

There will be a showdown on supranationalism after this war. The bitter debate between isolation and intervention (a debate ended abruptly last Sunday morning on an island in the Pacific) was really an extension of the fundamental conflict between the national spirit (which is in practically everyone) and the universal spirit (which is in some but not in all). Nationalism has two fatal charms for its devotees: it presupposes local self-sufficiency, which is a pleasant and desirable condition, and it suggests, very subtly, a certain personal superiority by reason of one's belonging to a place that is definable and familiar, as against a place that is strange, remote.

* * *

Before you can be a supranationalist you have first to be a naturalist and feel the ground under you making a whole circle. It is easier for a man to be loyal to his club than to his planet; the by-laws are shorter, and he is personally acquainted with the other members. A club, moreover, or a nation, has a most attractive offer to make: it offers the right to be exclusive. There are not many of us who are physically constituted to resist this strange delight, this nourishing privilege. It is at the bottom of all fraternities, societies, orders. It is at the bottom of most trouble. The planet holds out no such inducement. The planet is everybody's. All it offers is the grass, the sky, the water, and the ineluctable dream of peace and fruition.

Clubs, fraternities, nations—these are the beloved barriers in the way of a workable world, these will have to surrender some of their rights and some of their ribs. A "fraternity" is the antithesis of *fraternity*. The first (that is, the order or organization) is predicated on the idea of exclusion; the second (that is, the abstract thing) is based on a feeling of total equality. Anyone who remembers back to his fraternity days at college recalls the enthusiasts in his group, the rabid members, both old and young, who were obsessed with the mystical charm of membership in their particular order. They were usually men who were incapable of genuine brotherhood, or at least unaware of its implications. Fraternity begins when the exclusion formula is found to be distasteful. The effect of any organization of a social and brotherly nature is to strengthen rather than diminish the lines that divide people into classes; the effect of states and nations is the same, and eventually these lines will have to be softened, these powers will have to be generalized. It is written on the wall that this is so. I'm not inventing it, I'm just copying it off the wall.

I find, on rigid introspection, that my feeling for supranationalism, and my trust in it, are intuitive rather than reasonable. It is not so much that I have faith in the ability of nations to organize themselves as that I mistrust what will happen if again they fail to do so.

A book that has given me great pleasure during the past year is, in its delicate way, a shining advertisement of the universal spirit and a testimonial to its soundness. It is a book of folk songs called *Lullabies of Many Lands*, collected and arranged by Dorothy Berliner Commins. It contains sixteen songs that belong to sixteen peoples. These are beautiful songs and excellent arrangements, and they suggest a very strong and striking kinship among people everywhere. One of the loveliest is the German "*Schlaf, Kindlein, schlaf. Der Vater hüt't die Schaf Die Mutter Schuttelt's Bäumelein, Da fällt herab ein Träumelein. Schlaf, Kindlein, schlaf.*" I don't know what particular revision the minister of propaganda has given this lovely song, but I doubt if he can permanently alter or destroy the emotions that make it live. The more brutal and desperate the time, the steadier burns the belief in universal peace. The Chinese song tells the promise: "From the flute new music comes."

I think a good many people, here and everywhere, have a feeling in their bones that some sort of large-scale reawakening is in the cards for humanity. Intimations of this feeling are in the air—in the talk of the philosophers, in the speeches of the politicians, in the songs of the poets, in the wall charts of the economists. There is the vague feeling that after great evil comes great good; after trouble comes absence of trouble; after war, peace. It is a mystical, rather than a logical, presentiment. History does not offer any very impressive corroboration; flip over its pages and you are apt to find the disagreeable reminder that after trouble comes more trouble. Yet it is a feeling everyone must hold to.

Along with this presentiment, this hunch, goes the feeling that it is nip and tuck now with mankind on earth. Science, the dispassionate, has enabled the Japanese to deliver a terrible blow to the English and American fleets. Science, astride the fence, may enable our side to hit back. It all seems so delicately balanced. Nip we win, tuck we lose. The canny and careful reconstruction of barbarism, against the defense of old liberties and ideas. Life more and more seems to present itself in antithetical poses. Even radio news programs suggest the battle of the extremes: the world's largest-selling beauty soap paving the way for five minutes of the world's widest-spread predicament, the soft hands of Walter Winchell's lotion clasped against the tough heart of his defense of American freedom, fifteen minutes of a pleasure gasoline sponsorship in a war in which gasoline is almost the same as blood.

The mechanics and spirit of a capitalistic press and radio are both comical and beautiful today. The first words I heard after the news came of Japan's attack in Hawaii were: "Give Mother foot comfort for Christmas." It was in the voice we all know so well—as though the speaker had marshmallows in place of tonsils—but it had that thoroughly cockeyed quality for which in the long run we are fighting. It makes a man suddenly realize his strange and wonderful indebtedness to the cosmetic industry and the tobacco trade and all the rest that are supplying us with capsules of news every few moments.

I was in Washington a while ago, sniffing around and annoying people by looking into their wastebaskets; and while I was there I went over one morning to a Senate committee hearing where Mr. La Guardia [Fiorello La Guardia, three-term mayor of New York City from 1934 to 1945] was testifying. The committee was investigating the problem of small business men who were being squeezed out of business by defense rulings. It wasn't big news by a long shot, but a couple of cameramen showed up and maneuvered into position quietly, crouching one on either side of the Little Flower. They were well behaved, for photographers, but now and again one of them would explode a flash. Finally one of the committeemen spoke sharply, asked them to quit and let the hearing proceed in peace. They seemed not to hear this request. They just crouched, motionless. Then the Mayor asked them to go away and wait for him outside. The boys crouched and smiled. A newspaper correspondent sitting next to me said, proudly: "They won't pay any attention to those guys." Nothing was done. The hearing proceeded. It was a familiar pantomime—the free press, deplored yet admired. Under their vests the senators were secretly glad that they were unable to dislodge a couple of American photographers. It was what the hearing was about really—the photographers, squatting imperturbably in front of the men who were plotting to win a war that would preserve for photographers the right to squat imperturbably.

It is hard to believe now that Washington was ever the way I saw it a week or so before the outbreak of war. I had been told that I should find Washington a madhouse, but I remember it as a quiet place that managed somehow to give the impression of stability and peace, no matter how rapidly the bureaus were proliferating. Nobody seemed worried. The taxi driver who took me from the station to the hotel said he was on his way the next morning to apply for a time-keeping job on a defense project, which would pay fifty dollars a week; and he reported with considerable enthusiasm that some of the laborers on the job had made as high as one hundred and six dollars in one week. Not even a collapsing world looks dark to a man who is about to make his fortune. The President, when he received the press in his Oval Study, gave little sign of tension and went out of his way to capture a joke or a pleasantry in midair. The weather was soft and agreeable; in the parks the oaks still held their leaves, releasing one now and then, indolently. Young girls on their hard high heels tapped home from the offices through the warm benign parks, and the squirrels and the pigeons deployed in the sunlight. In the Maryland countryside, where I visited for a weekend, there was the same hazy beauty, somnolence, and security—the little firm hills and the valleys between, friendly and warm as a mother's lap, the cornstalks in the still green pastures, the big barns, the winter wheat, and the honeysuckle and the cedars and the holly. In the morning the birds struck up almost as cheerfully as in the deep South, and on the air was the skunky smell of box. Here and there the physical signs of war, nowhere the conviction of its reality.

The whole history of the war so far has been the inability of people in the democracies to believe their eyes and ears. They didn't believe the Rhineland or the persecution of the Jews or Poland or France or any of the rest of it. That phase of the war is over. Now, at least, we can see and hear.

Treason, Defined
(When Congress Delays an Issue)

Treason is too narrowly interpreted to suit us. Our courts call it treason when a restaurant-keeper helps a German flier to escape, but nobody calls it treason when a congressman helps a touchy issue to escape "until after the elections are over." We hang a man for the first kind of treason; we reelect a man for the second. This is the summer, of all summers, when the world will learn just how far treason can go and still stay clear of the noose. This is the summer when time is the most precious thing there is—more precious than rubber or metal or men. Yet some of our political leaders are throwing time around as though it were confetti. Who is the greater traitor, anyway, a man with a German flier concealed in his cellar or a man with a national issue buried in his portfolio?

It is not only treacherous to help the enemy by postponing questions which involve the lives of all of us but it is the greatest insult which can be offered to the electorate of a democracy. When you hear it announced that such-and-such an issue cannot be raised now because it is "political dynamite," the implication

is that you yourself are mixed up in a cheap trick per-
petrated by one section of the people on another sec-
tion. This doesn't happen to be a summer when we
feel like being insulted. We happen to be a little edgy
this summer—we won't take much more of that sort
of insult.

Crackpots

We noticed, with some misgivings, that the American Federation of Teachers put out a warning the other day that there would be no "crackpots" admitted to its membership. Only those teachers would be admitted who would be a credit to the Federation and instill in boys and girls an abiding loyalty to the ideals and principles of democracy. But as we understand it, one of the noblest attributes of democracy is that it contains no one who can truthfully say, of two pots, which is the cracked, which is the whole. That is basic. The Federation better welcome all comers, and let pot clink against pot.

Education is such a serious matter, we speak of it with trepidation. We remember, with sober and contrite heart, that our educational system was responsible for (among others) the group of citizens who for two years did everything in their power to prove that the war which was going on did not involve us, that nothing was happening abroad which was of any consequence in our lives, that the earth was not round. Those people—millions of them—were all educated in American schools by non-crackpots. They were brought up on American curricula. They damn near did us in.

They are ready again to do us in, as soon as an opening presents itself—which will be immediately after hostilities cease. On the basis of the record, it would seem that we need what crackpots we can muster for education in our new world. We need educators who believe that character is more precious than special knowledge, that vision is not just something arrived at through a well-ground lens, and that a child is the most hopeful (and historically the most neglected) property the Republic boasts.

The Meaning of Democracy

We received a letter from the Writers' War Board the other day asking for a statement on "The Meaning of Democracy." It presumably is our duty to comply with such a request, and it is certainly our pleasure.

Surely the Board knows what democracy is. It is the line that forms on the right. It is the don't in don't shove. It is the hole in the stuffed shirt through which the sawdust slowly trickles; it is the dent in the high hat. Democracy is the recurrent suspicion that more than half of the people are right more than half of the time. It is the feeling of privacy in the voting booths, the feeling of communion in the libraries, the feeling of vitality everywhere. Democracy is a letter to the editor. Democracy is the score at the beginning of the ninth. It is an idea which hasn't been disproved yet, a song the words of which have not gone bad. It's the mustard on the hot dog and the cream in the rationed coffee. Democracy is a request from a War Board, in the middle of a morning in the middle of a war, wanting to know what democracy is.

Definition of Fascism

It is already apparent that the word "Fascist" will be one of the hardest-worked words in the Presidential campaign. Henry Wallace called some people Fascists the other day in a speech and next day up jumped Harrison Spangler, the Republican, to remark that if there were any Fascists in this country you would find them in the New Deal's palace guard. It is getting so a Fascist is a man who votes the other way. Persons who vote *your* way, of course, continue to be "right-minded people."

We are sorry to see this misuse of the word "Fascist." If we recall matters, a Fascist is a member of the Fascist party or a believer in Fascist ideals. These are: a nation founded on bloodlines, political expansion by surprise and war, murder or detention of unbelievers, transcendence of state over individual, obedience to one leader, contempt for parliamentary forms, plus some miscellaneous gymnastics for the young and a general feeling of elation. It seems to us that there are many New Deal Democrats who do not subscribe to such a program, also many aspiring Republicans. Other millions of Americans are nonsubscribers. It's too bad to emasculate the word "Fascist" by using it on persons whose only offense is that they vote the wrong ticket. The word should be saved for use in cases where it applies, as it does to members of our Ku Klux Klan, for instance, whose beliefs and practices are identical with Fascism.

Unfortunately (or perhaps fortunately), there is a certain quality in Fascism which is quite close to a certain quality in nationalism. Fascism is openly against people-in-general, in favor of people-in-particular. Nationalism, although in theory not dedicated to such an idea, actually works against people-in-general because of its preoccupation with people-in-particular. It reminds one of Fascism, also, in its determination to stabilize its own position by whatever haphazard means present themselves—by treaties, policies, balances, agreements, pacts, and the jockeying for position which is summed up in the term "diplomacy." This doesn't make an America Firster a Fascist. It simply makes him, in our opinion, a man who hasn't grown into his pants yet. The persons who have written most persuasively against nationalism are the young soldiers who have got far enough from our shores to see the amazing implications of a planet. Once you see it, you never forget it.

Preface to *The Wild Flag* (excerpted here)

. . . A recurrent theme of the book [*The Wild Flag*] is world government, as distinct from the sort of international league which is now functioning under the name "United Nations." The most persistent criticism of world government is that although it may be a laudable idea, to discuss it is futile, even harmful, since there is no means of achieving it at present. This criticism may be valid. Certainly nobody, not even an editorial writer, can quite figure how a world government could be set up when two of the biggest nations are operating under political systems which seem irreconcilable. But I believe that the case for a unified world is worth stating theoretically at any time. The answer to war is no war. And the likeliest means of removing war from the routine of national life is to elevate the community's authority to a level which is above national level. This, in fact, is the destination toward which the human seems to be drifting, in violence and in pain; it should also be the goal toward which our statesmen are pointing, and I am afraid it seldom is. Much of the political construction which is being carried on in the name of humanity is still strictly limited to the national conception of human affairs. The first thing a draftsman does, when he prepares a charter, is to lock his country's sovereignty up in the safe so that nobody can tamper with it.

Nationalism is young and strong, and has already run into bad trouble. We take pains to educate our children at an early age in the rituals and mysteries of the nation, infusing national feeling into them in place of the universal feeling which is their birthright; but lately the most conspicuous activity of nations has been the blowing of each other up, and an observant child might reasonably ask whether he is pledging allegiance to a flag or to a shroud. A nation asks of its citizens everything—their fealty, their money, their faith, their time, their lives. It is fair to ask whether the nation, in return, does indeed any longer serve the best interests of the human beings who give so lavishly of their affections and their blood. We know, we Americans, what America means in the human heart; we remember its principles and we honor its record; but we tend to forget that it has its counterpart in sixty or seventy other places. This is mischievous business. It is bloody business. Reinforced with the atom, it may be fatal business.

Whether we wish it or not, we may soon have to make a clear choice between the special nation to which we pledge our allegiance and the broad humanity of which we are born a part. This choice is implicit in the world to come. We have a little time in which we can make the choice intelligently. Failing that, the choice will be made for us in the confusion of war, from which the world will emerge unified—the unity of total desolation.

The anatomy of loyalty is largely unexplored. Yet it is a branch of social science which suggests exciting discoveries for the long future. If the range of our planes continues to increase, the range of our thoughts will have to increase or there will be none of us left to do the thinking, and the focus of our allegiance will have to shift or we will find ourselves at last with nothing left to be loyal to. A world government, were we ever to get one, would impose on the individual the curious burden of taking the entire globe to his bosom—although not in any sense depriving him of the love of his front yard. The special feeling of an Englishman for a special stream in Devonshire or a lane in Kent would have to run parallel to his pride in Athens and his insane love of Jersey City. The special feeling of a Netherlander for a dyke in Holland would have to extend onward and outward until it found the Norris Dam and the terraces of Egypt. A Chinese farmer in a rice paddy would have to feel, between his toes, not only the immediate wetness of his own field, but the vast wetness of the fertile world. A world made one, by the political union of its parts, would not only require of its citizen a shift of allegiance, but it would deprive him of the enormous personal satisfaction of distrusting what he doesn't know and despising what he hasn't seen. This would be a severe deprivation, perhaps an intolerable one. The awful truth is, a world government would lack an enemy, and that is a deficiency not to be lightly dismissed. It will take a yet undiscovered vitamin to supply the blood of man with a substitute for national ambition and racial antipathy; but we are discovering new vitamins all the time, and I am aware of that, too.

Two things in the human scene give encouragement to anyone who takes to brooding on these matters. For one thing, a cosmopolis is a fairly common sight. A big city is a noisy proof of man's ability to live at peace with strangers, with newcomers, and with what he blithely calls the "objectionable elements." The City of New York is a world government on a small scale. There, truly, is the world in a nutshell, its citizens meeting in the subway, and ballpark, sunning on the benches in the square. They shove each other, but seldom too hard. They annoy each other, but rarely to the point of real trouble. There Greek and German work and pray, there Pole and Russian eat and dance. They enjoy the peace that goes with government, and the police are beautiful to behold. Any big city should be an important exhibit in the laboratory where the anatomy of loyalty is under investigation—and we had better not delay, either, for big cities are not as numerous as they were a few years ago. Some of them have turned up missing.

The other encouraging thing is that war is becoming increasingly unpopular with warriors. We needn't set too much store by this; nevertheless, it is stimulating to learn that the ones that have been doing the fighting have an extremely low opinion of the whole business. If war were only mildly unpopular, one might despair of ever getting rid of it down the drain. But war has reached a new low in the esteem of all people. The bombing of cities has made every citizen a participant in war, and this has swelled the ranks of war's detractors.

As for these editorials, they were written sometimes in anger and always in haste. They will be too purely theoretical for the practicing statesman, who is faced with the grim job of operating with equipment at hand, and too sweetly reasonable for the skeptic, who knows what an unpredictable customer the human being is. (A worker in the next stall has just informed me that world government is impractical because "there are too many Orientals.") But theory and sweet reason are all right in their place; and if these topical paragraphs add an ounce to the long-continuing discussion of nationalism, and throw even as much as a flashlight's gleam on the wild flag which our children, and their children, must learn to know and love, I am satisfied.

No Fooling

There is now a demand that Nazi leaders be "tried and punished" for all crimes back as far as 1933. Yet the cold truth is there is not a Nazi living who can be tried or brought to justice for anything he has done, because we have no justice to bring him to. To talk of justice as though it were something you could pull out of a hat, as occasion requires, is to talk idly and badly. When a German officer tortures and butchers the innocent people of a village, he can be caught and shot by firing squad (and we trust he will be), but he cannot be brought to justice. The only way you can try and punish an individual who has committed an antisocial act on an international level is by setting up shop on that level, creating the courts on that level, writing the laws on that level, and supporting the enforcement on that level. Whether people want to set up shop on that level, whether people are capable of it, whether it is wise to attempt it—these are questions still unanswered by the democratic nations. Our private hope is that the answer will be Yes, but until the people make up their minds they ought to keep the record clean and not kid themselves about jurisdiction and crime. You can't have your anarchical society and eat it, too.

One of the so-called crimes the Germans committed eleven years ago was the burning of books in public—a universal gesture of contempt for the free circulation of human ideas. Such an act was incipient aggression and was on the level we've been talking about. Query: Does the world want a law prohibiting an individual from burning books in public? Query: Does it want a law prohibiting a fanatical German or a fanatical Anybody from murdering innocent villagers? Query: Does it want a law, applicable to all people, which says, "Thou shall not spit in thy neighbor's eye"? You can answer these questions any way you like, but you can't pretend that that sort of justice is here yet. The road leading to it is a long, tough one, and we haven't even started up it. The league structure proposed at Dumbarton Oaks does not seem to us to lead toward the goal (except in spirit), since a league is mere caricature of government, with nations attempting to judge nations and the individual left out of the picture. Our belief is that the way lies through a federation of democratic countries, which differs from a league in that it has a legislature that can legislate, a judiciary that can judge, and an executive that can execute. It does not have to operate through diplomacy, and it has a No Fooling sign on the door.

Bill of Human Rights

It is wonderful news that a Bill of Human Rights will be submitted at the peace parley. Such a guarantee, however, in order to be effective, would necessitate a change in the proposed world-peace structure. Human rights take shape and meaning when they are associated with representative government involving responsibility and duty. So far, the peace proposals do not include popular representation in the council and the assembly, and the people therefore assume no personal responsibility for anything and therefore will gain no personal rights. Commissions (stop us if we are wrong about this) cannot create human rights.

Mrs. Roosevelt apparently does not want anyone to write stuff like the paragraph above. In a recent column she expressed the fear that "perfectionists" would wreck the chances of getting some kind of peace organization through the Senate. "Those who cannot compromise should be looked down upon by their neighbors," she wrote. We have been going on the assumption that during the period of the preliminary peace talk, it is a citizen's function to air his opinions and instruct his delegates according to his lights. We intend to go to work on the Senate and urge it to join in world affairs when the Senate itself has something to go to work on. Meantime, we will continue to believe that although a man may have to compromise with Russia he can never compromise with truth. Our neighbors can look down; the top of our head is not much of a sight.

We are perfectionist to the extent that we regard this world as an imperfect one and consequently in need of the best possible government of law, order, and human rights based on human responsibilities. To us, a perfectionist is someone who wants another man's neighbors to look down on him for having an opinion.

Right to Work

Russia's collectivist system and our own individualist system are incapable of being reconciled by a girl's kiss, but every once in a while Congress seems about to reconcile them by bestowing the kiss of death on private enterprise. We see by the papers that the Senate has decided that we ought to "guarantee" profits to farmers and has adopted the Wherry amendment to that effect. And lately there has been talk in the highest circles of the "right to work" or the "right to a job." Such ideas are essentially collectivist, and any country which assumes that it can guarantee its profits and make them, too, is probably living in a dream.

Commissar Molotov included a "right to work" clause when he submitted proposals for the Dumbarton Oaks plan, thereby getting in a plug for state control. President Roosevelt, we recall, once used the phrase "right to work" in a speech, and it seemed to us at the time that the issue was becoming rapidly confused. In this country, the citizens have never enjoyed the *right* to work, and until recently it has not occurred to any considerable numbers of them that they wanted any such thing. Instead, they have settled for the right to look for work, the right to decent working conditions, the right to haggle about pay, the right to equality of opportunity, the right to a fair trial when they are arrested for drunkenness that sometimes follows unemployment, the right to pan the government, and the special right of veterans to be taken back into jobs. We rather doubt that those fundamental American conceptions are reconcilable with the over-all "right to work." And we suspect that as soon as you attempt to endow the profit system with a guarantee of profits, you have presumably removed the system itself.

Never having been in Russia, we don't know what it's like there. But our guess is that there are as many confusions in the Russian mind about the alluring attributes of capitalism that must crop up in a Communist state as there are confusions over here about the attractive guarantees and rights and controls of our private economy. Someday Russia and the United States will participate in a common government of some sort, along with other nations, and then people can begin to scramble their ideologies in the same skillet and to enjoy the best features of both systems. Luckily, people the world over want approximately the same thing: kisses, bread, and a chance to get in out of the rain. They even want peace, most of them.

International Justice System

In Wiesbaden, the other day, seven Germans went on trial for the wholesale murder of some slave workers—Poles and Russians, mostly, who had been put to death for reasons which suited Germany at that particular moment. The trial was conducted by United States officers. According to an account we read of it in the *Times*, the defense attorney, an American, challenged the legal basis of the trial and quoted *The New Yorker* to support his argument. Thus this magazine, in the minds of some, will appear to be the friend of murderers, the bedfellow of beasts. Despite this difficult role, we stick to our story, and for what we hope is a good reason. The two things which seem vital to us at this point are, first, that the criminals rounded up after a war should be promptly punished for their deeds, and, second, that the special procedure for inflicting such punishment should be clearly admitted to be extralegal and not palmed off on the world as run-of-the-mill justice. For an American court to hang a German who murdered a Russian during a war is completely outside any legal system that we know anything about, and we believe that it is quite important to state this and not try to obscure it.

The need for a broader justice for men, the need for a broader scheme of life than exists today, is great, and the first step toward constructing it is to recognize its absence. These so-called war trials can be magnificent if they can be made to clarify rather than cloud this issue; they will be extremely valuable as precedents if they are presented as a preview of the justice that may someday exist, not as an example of the justice that we have on hand. We are in favor of the higher level of law by which victorious Americans now seek to punish vanquished Germans for murdering captive Russian slaves. We hope the United Nations organizations will catch up with the hard-riding lawyers of Wiesbaden, who are way out in front. Nobody, not even victors, should forget that when a man hangs from a tree it doesn't spell justice unless he helped write the law that hanged him.

Pearl Harbor Investigation

The senators bark at the wrong tree.
The cause of war? 'Twas caused by me.
Blame saturates the earth like dew.
The cause of war? 'Twas caused by you.

To prove that someone was asleep
The senators probe long and deep,
And, backward peering through the mist,
Each proves himself somnambulist.

Instructions to a Delegate

Make an original and four copies, Miss Eberhard, one for each delegate. A delegate, on his way to assembly, carries two sets of instructions: one dictated by his own conscience (but not read) and one handed him by his constituents. Herewith we hand to each delegate to the first assembly of the United Nations Organization his instructions:

When you sit down, sit down as an American if it makes you feel comfortable, but when you rise to speak, get up like a man anywhere.

Do not bring home any bacon; it will have turned rancid on the journey. Bring home instead a silken thread, by which you may find your way back.

Bear in mind always that foreign policy is domestic policy with its hat on. The purpose of the meeting, although not so stated anywhere, is to replace policy with law, and to make common sense.

Make common sense.

Think not to represent us by safeguarding our interests. Represent us by perceiving that our interests are other people's, and theirs ours.

When you think with longing of the place where you were born, remember that the sun leaves it daily to go somewhere else. When you think with love of America, think of the impurity of its bloodlines and of how no American ever won a prize in a dog show.

Carry good men with you in your portfolio, along with the order of the day. Read the men with the short first names: Walt Whitman, John Donne, Manny Kant, Abe Lincoln, Tom Paine, Al Einstein. Read them and weep. Then read them again, without tears.

If you would speak up for us, do not speak up for America, speak up for people, for the free man. We are not dispatching you to build national greatness. Unless you understand this and believe it, you might better be at the race track, where you can have a good time simply by guessing wrong.

Never forget that the nature of peace is commonly misstated. Peace is not to be had by preventing aggression, for it is always too late for that. Peace is to be had when people's antagonisms and antipathies are subject to the discipline of law and the decency of government.

Do not try to save the world by loving thy neighbor; it will only make him nervous. Save the world by respecting thy neighbor's rights under law and insisting that he respect yours (under the same law). In short, save the world.

Observe that Chapter IV, Article II, Paragraph 3 of the Charter asks the General Assembly to "call the attention of the Security Council to situations which are likely to endanger international peace and security." We instruct you, accordingly, to call the Council's attention to the one situation which most consistently endangers peace: absolute national sovereignty. Remind the Council of the frailty, the insubstantiality, of your own Organization, in which members are not people but states.

Do not be confused by the noise of the atomic bomb. The bomb is the pea shooter come home to roost. But when you dream, dream of essential matters, of mass-energy relationships, of man-man relationships. The scientists have outdreamed you, little delegate, so dream well.

Be concerned with principles, not with results. We do not ask for results, merely for a soil-building program. You are not at a chess game, even though it has the appearance of one; you are at a carnival of hope.

For bedside reading we prescribe the opening remarks of Justice Jackson at the Nuremberg trial: "The idea that a State, any more than a corporation, commits crimes is a fiction. Crimes always are committed only by persons." (Yet the U.N.O. has been chartered to stop states from committing crimes.) And further: ". . . that fictional being, 'the State,' which cannot be produced for trial, cannot plead, cannot testify, and cannot be sentenced." We instruct you to compare these words with Chapter II of the Charter, which says that the members of your Organization are states. If, as Justice Jackson points out, your membership is a fiction, then your first task should be to become more factual, less fictional. Your task will be to introduce people into the pie. Eventually you will have to supplant states with people, policy with law, diplomacy with legality, internationalism with federal union, and you probably haven't as much time as you like to think you have.

As talisman, do not carry a colored flag for the special occasion; carry a white handkerchief for the common cold. Blow your nose frequently and listen to the universal sound.

Finally, now that the Emperor has disclaimed divinity, we charge you to believe in yourself and to love truth. Build the great republic. The foundation is inescapable. The foundation is unity. It is what your initials suggest: UNO.

Spy System

It would appear that Russia has been spying on Canada—a bit of news which seemed to come as a surprise to everyone. We heard one commentator say that the spy story in Canada was "as good as a mystery thriller." We didn't think it was anywhere near as good as a mystery thriller. If there is one thing which no longer should remain mysterious to anyone, or thrilling, it is that every nation must of necessity spy on every other nation. How else can a nation get information which it needs concerning the habits, plans, and secrets of other nations? Spying is not a mystery. To us it is far from thrilling: it is putrefactive.

As a child we played a game called I Spy. As a man, we are fully aware that we live in a society which plays that game, for its life. It plays it because it has always played it and because it hasn't worked out the rules of any other game. Every year the stakes grow higher, the game grows rougher. Soon the barn will fall on the children. If Americans and Canadians grow indignant at Russia for stealing atomic information, they are being innocent beyond belief. If the United States is not at this moment spying on fifty or sixty other nations, to find out what is going on inside their borders, then it is not only innocent, it is derelict. If fifty or sixty other nations are not operating inside the United States, then those other nations are derelict, too. A nation that doesn't spy today is not giving its people an even break.

If there is any sentiment among people to abandon the spy system and get on to something forthright, we recommend that they instruct their U.N.O. delegates to get busy on the project. At the moment we are headed not toward but away from it—strengthening national lines and turning global problems over to commissions. Atomic energy will never be controlled by commission. Human rights will never be established by commission. A free press and the right to know will never become universal by commission. Peace is expensive, and so are human rights and civil liberties; they have a price, and we the peoples have not yet offered to pay it. Instead we are trying to furnish our globe with these precious ornaments the cheap way, holding our sovereignty cautiously in one fist while extending the other hand in a gesture of cooperation. In the long run, this will prove the hard way, the violent way. The United Nations Organization, which in its present form is a league of disunited nations whose problems are on the table and whose spies are behind the arras, is our last chance to substitute order for disorder, government for anarchy, knowledge for espionage. We better make it good. Remember, an intelligence service is, in fact, a stupidity service; if we were really intelligent, we wouldn't be willing to stake our children's lives on our country's spies.

(The Importance of)
Many Newspaper Owners

The question of a free press came up in a roundabout way during *PM*'s change of editors. [Ralph Ingersoll's *PM* (1940–1948) was a liberal-leaning newspaper run without advertising, though it was largely financed by Chicago millionaire Marshall Field III.] Mr. Ingersoll, resigning, did not charge that if a paper accepted ads it couldn't be free; he merely said that "there should be at least one mass newspaper in this country supported solely by its readers." We have often wondered why it is so difficult to publish such a paper. One of the odd things about advertising (and there are many odd things about it) is that the public rather counts on it. We found that out during the war, when we sent an edition overseas with no ads. The boys complained that they were being shortchanged. Our guess is that an adless newspaper, to succeed, would have to be unquestionably superior in every department to the kept press. Short of that (and *PM* was short of it), an adless paper is licked. There is a quality in advertising, quite aside from the way it pays the bills, which seems peculiarly to complement reading matter; a certain extravagance of phrase, an unreality, a rhinestone brilliance, an unworldliness, and a promise. The ads are the reader's dream life, the reading matter is his waking hour. We suspect he loves them both. After a column of pure thought, a half page of crunchy goodness; after a hard editorial, a brand-new helicopter, easy to own and operate.

A free press is in a healthy condition when there are plenty of owners. We don't care whether *PM* takes ads or doesn't take ads. What we do care about is that *PM* shall continue to get published. In England, where the ownership of the press is now under investigation, the question is not whether there are "lords of the press"; the question is whether there are enough of them. A writer in the New York *Times* made light of the inquiry, pointing out that the people, both in England and in America, don't always vote the way the press tells them to, and therefore it doesn't make any difference about combines and mergers. This misses the point, it seems to us. The majority of the voters may not always go along with the majority press opinion, but if there are enough owners of enough papers, the people at least have access to the whole range of fact and opinion, not just to part of it. Then what they decide to do is based on information, not on mysticism.

Love Among the Foreign Offices

Moscow, Jan. 23—The claim first made on January 15 that Foreign Secretary Bevin of Britain renounced the Anglo-Soviet treaty of alliance in his speech on December 22 was defended today by *Pravda*, official organ of the Communist party.

—*THE TIMES*

STALIN UPHOLDS BRITISH TIE . . . SERIOUS RIFT HELD AVERTED.

—*THE TIMES*, JANUARY 25

"England, do you love me?"
   Said Russia to her love.
"Of course I love you, Sweetie
Let's sign a treaty!"
   (They loved each other so,
   But that was months ago.)

"You love me not," says Russia.
   "I saw you look at France."
"How quite absurd," says England.
   "That was the merest glance."

"You love me not," says Russia.
   "You're treating me like dirt;

It's all come out in *Pravda*—
    You're just a common flirt."

"Oh, false words, false words," says England.
    "I love you most sincerely;
You *know* I love you, Sweetie,
It says so in the treaty.
    I love you dearly.
        It makes me gloomy
        When you misconstrue me."

Russia:
"By heaven, listen to Bevin!
    Have I not ears and eyes?
    He said you have no ties.
Clearly you love me not."

"I love you *so,*" says England
    "You love me not," says R.
"I do!"
    "You don't!"
"I do!"
    "You don't!"
"I *do.* You go too far."

"O.K., you do," says Stalin.
"But watch that ring,
You promiscuous thing!"

(So runs the love of nations
  As old men specify—
The fitful love of nations,
  For which the young men die.)

Dwindling Ownership of the Press

[New York]

March 10, 1947

Dear Mr. Wentworth:

I still think the American press informs the people, not completely and not without bias, but informs them. I was simply comparing it with a truly kept press where nobody gets any information at all.

I think that it is not so much the relationship between business office and editorial office that should worry people in a democracy as it is the dwindling of ownership of the press. As [long as] there are a lot of papers and a lot of owners I think the news gets out, even news such as you complain about. . . .

Sincerely,

E. B. White

Herald Tribune ("Hollywood Ten" Letters)

In an editorial published on November 27, 1947, the *Herald Tribune*, though somewhat grudgingly, supported the right of the movie industry to blacklist the "Hollywood Ten" and any others who refused to answer questions before J. Parnell Thomas's House Un-American Activities Committee. The following letter, White's reaction to the editorial, was published in the *Tribune* on December 2.

New York, New York

November 29, 1947

To the New York *Herald Tribune*:

I am a member of a party of one, and I live in an age of fear. Nothing lately has unsettled my party and raised my fears so much as your editorial, on Thanksgiving Day, suggesting that employees should be required to state their beliefs in order to hold their jobs. The idea is inconsistent with our Constitutional theory and has been stubbornly opposed by watchful men since the early days of the Republic. It's hard for me to believe that the *Herald Tribune* is backing away from the fight, and I can only assume that your editorial writer, in a hurry to get home for

Thanksgiving, tripped over the First Amendment and
thought it was the office cat.

The investigation of alleged Communists by the
Thomas committee has been a confusing spectacle
for all of us. I believe its implications are widely
misunderstood and that the outcome is grave beyond
exaggerating. The essence of our political theory in
this country is that a man's conscience shall be a
private, not a public affair, and that only his deeds
and words shall be open to survey, censure and to
punishment. The idea is a decent one, and it works.
It is an idea that cannot safely be compromised with,
lest it be utterly destroyed. It cannot be modified even
under circumstances where, for security reasons, the
temptation to modify it is great.

I think security in critical times takes care of
itself if the people and the institutions take care of
themselves. First in line is the press. Security, for
me, took a tumble not when I read that there were
Communists in Hollywood but when I read your
editorial in praise of loyalty testing and thought
control. If a man is in health, he doesn't need to take
anybody else's temperature to know where he is going.
If a newspaper or a motion picture company is in
health, it can get rid of Communists and spies simply
by reading proof and by watching previews.

I hold that it would be improper for any committee
or any employer to examine my conscience. They
wouldn't know how to get into it, they wouldn't know

what to do when they got in there, and I wouldn't let them in anyway. Like other Americans, my acts and my words are open to inspection—not my thoughts or my political affiliation. (As I pointed out, I am a member of a party of one.) Your editorialist said he hoped the companies in checking for loyalty would use their powers sparingly and wisely. That is a wistful idea. One need only watch totalitarians at work to see that once men gain power over other men's minds, that power is never used sparingly and wisely, but lavishly and brutally and with unspeakable results. If I must declare today that I am not a Communist, tomorrow I shall have to testify that I am not a Unitarian. And the day after, that I never belonged to a dahlia club.

It is not a crime to believe anything at all in America. To date it has not been declared illegal to belong to the Communist party. Yet ten men have been convicted not of wrongdoing but of wrong believing. That is news in this country, and if I have not misread history, it is bad news.

E. B. White

On the same page on the same day that White's November 29 letter was published in the *Tribune*, another editorial appeared, entitled, "The Party of One." It said that people such as Mr. White "have been with us since the dawn of civilization. They have always been highly valuable elements in our civilization and nearly always as destructive as they have been valuable." Members of the party of one were also characterized as "probably the most dangerous single elements in our confused and complicated society."

White's reply to the "Party of One" editorial appeared on December 9, under the heading "Mr. White Believes Us Needlessly Unkind."

New York

December 4, 1947

To the New York *Herald Tribune*:

The editorial that you wrote about me illustrated what I meant about the loyalty check system and about what would happen if it got going in the industrial world. My letter, expressing a dissenting opinion, was a letter that any conscientious reader might write to his newspaper, and you answered it by saying I belonged to "probably the most dangerous element in our society." Thus a difference of opinion became suddenly a mark of infamy. A man who disagreed with a *Tribune* editorial used to be called plucky—now he's called dangerous. By your own definition I already belong among the unemployables.

You said that in these times we need "new concepts and new principles" to combat subversion. It seems to me the loyalty check in industry is not a new principle at all. It is like the "new look," which is really the old, old look, slightly tinkered up. The principle of

demanding an expression of political conformity
as the price of a job is the principle of hundred
percentism. It is not new and it is blood brother of
witch burning.

I don't know why I should be bawling out the
Herald Tribune or why the *Herald Tribune* should
be bawling out me. I read those Bert Andrews pieces
and got a new breath of fresh air. Then I turned in
a dissenting opinion about an editorial and got hit
over the head with a stick of wood. These times are
too edgy. It is obvious to everyone that the fuss about
loyalty arises from fear of war with Russia, and from
the natural feeling that we should clear our decks of
doubtful characters. Well, I happen to believe that we
can achieve reasonably clear decks if we continue to
apply our civil rights and duties equally to all citizens,
even to citizens of opposite belief. That may be a
dangerous and false idea, but my holding it does not
necessarily make me a dangerous and false man, and
I wish that the *Herald Tribune* next time it sits down
to write a piece about me and my party would be good
enough to make the distinction. Right now it's a pretty
important distinction to make.

E. B. White

Determined to have the last word, the *Tribune* printed a
parenthetical editorial comment right underneath White's
letter. The comment began "Perhaps we were over-emphatic
in our disagreement with Mr. White, but since the same

editorial which suggested that he belonged to a 'dangerous element' also said that it was a 'highly valuable' element, he can scarcely hold that we were attaching any badge of 'infamy' to him." The editor went on to express the *Tribune*'s regard for White, to deny that its editors were the slightest bit afraid of war with Russia, and to state that they continued to feel that communism was "exploiting toleration in order to destroy toleration." The comment concluded that "We may be misguided in our attempts to deal with it, but it seems to us that Mr. White fails to deal with it at all."

[New York]

December 12, 1947

Dear Justice [Felix] Frankfurter:

There are more devils than angels around here at the moment, but I shall continue to give tongue. [Frankfurter's congratulatory letter to White about his exchange with the *Tribune* had contained the phrase "speak with the tongues of angels."] Your letter was most encouraging. My *Tribune* excursion into the realm of civil liberties covered me with a surprising lot of goat feathers, and I could hardly get my breath and needed a letter like yours.

Many thanks.

Very sincerely yours,

E. B. White

[New York]

December 15, 1947

Dear Mr. [Maurice] Zolotow:

Thanks for the letter—I'm a little late answering. It's true that I am not well informed on Communist Party maneuvers, but that's not the point. The point is whether we want the government to step into communications industries and start hiring and firing the employees. I'm against it, because I know where it leads. My editorial [*The New Yorker* "Notes and Comment" (12/6/47), a blast at the Hollywood producers who had fired ten writers in a loyalty purge] was not a commentary on the character, motives, or ability of the Hollywood men, it was a warning against industry surrendering its prerogatives to government, and allowing itself to decline to the point where it is incapable of running its own show.

I am firmly on your side about Communism, but I believe that in order to keep it in check, we must not stir the deep fears and hatreds of the American people and make suspects out of millions of innocent citizens. That is just exactly what the Communists are hoping we will do, if my guess is any good.

E. B. White

229 East 48 Street [New York]

January 24, 1948

Dear Bun [Stanley Hart White]:

Many thanks to you and Blanche for the Countryman's Companion. It seems to be a good collection. . . .

I have had a rather wild fall and winter so far, thanks to my incurable habit of putting practically anything that comes into my head down on paper and getting it published in newspapers and magazines. It is a lousy habit and I would be better off if I were a confirmed drunkard. I got into a little argument with the *Herald Tribune* on the subject of loyalty-checking, during which they ran an editorial about me saying that I belonged to the most dangerous element in society. I was delighted, as I had not known my own strength up till then. It seems that all you have to do to be tagged "dangerous" nowadays is to stand up for the First Amendment to the Constitution. Then I wrote an editorial in *The New Yorker* on the subject of the Hollywood purge and the Un-American Activities Committee, and I was soon getting courted by all the Communist front organizations. My desk got so deep in Red literature that I had to fumigate myself every night before going home. It was worse than athlete's foot. Then a piece of mine came out in the *Atlantic Monthly*, a simple rustic tale about the death of a

pig, and the *Ellsworth* (Maine) *American* attacked
it as malicious. You can't even come out against
constipation in America any more.

However, things in general are all right, and
my head feels rather better than it did a year ago.
There's not much news to report. Roger and Evelyn
had a baby girl a couple of weeks ago, and Roger
is supporting it by working for a magazine called
Holiday, a travel publication based on the perfectly
sound idea that everybody in the United States
would like to be somewhere else. Joe is working for
a construction company, helping remodel the *Times*
Annex. K still works like ten horses at *The New
Yorker*, but her spine is on the blink and gives her a lot
of bad trouble. I was interested in your review of the
Fifth Edition of *Webster's*. I own a copy inscribed "To
Stuart Little" from Robert C. Munroe, the president of
G. & C. Merriam Company.

Zoë mou, sas agapo [from a Lord Byron poem, and
meaning "My life, I love you"].

En

Loyalty

Hollywood handled the theme of loyalty the way it has handled most great themes—by avoiding it, by disregarding its subtle values, by perverting its meaning. The last act in the Waldorf, when the fifty top executives publicly sacked the ten condemned employees, set a precedent for the American purge. Every pen, every typewriter, reeled under the blow. It came a couple of days before Thanksgiving, when children were singing the words about the Pilgrim Fathers: "What sought they thus afar? . . . They have left unstained what there they found . . ." The theme was clearly too big for Hollywood, which has seldom left unstained what here it found and which has almost invariably shown itself incapable of dealing intelligently even with small themes.

Mr. Johnson said that the producers recognize that their policy of hiring and firing on a loyalty basis involves dangers and risks: "Creative work at its best cannot be carried on in an atmosphere of fear." Mr. Johnson was running ahead of his story. Why didn't he and the producers admit that it was fear that brought them to the Waldorf, fear that started the investigation, fear that led them to string along with the Thomas committee, whose right of inquiry is clear enough but whose technique is an abomination in a free country? As for writers being incapacitated by fear, the Hollywood incident of firing ten men for refusing to reveal their politics has already created plenty of atmospheric fear, but it may not have quite the effect the producers are worried about. Sometimes when a writer trembles all over he is more mad than scared. The most fearsome periods in America have produced some pretty good stuff, and may again. If the practice of inquiring into a man's beliefs becomes general, then every writer in America knows that the words he is writing today are the words he may swing for tomorrow. Not many of them will quit saying the words, even for twenty-five hundred dollars a week, the standard Hollywood wage.

What is loyalty? And to what shall a man be true? We can't help eyeing with suspicion the treatment of the theme of political loyalty by an industry whose artistic loyalty has been so yielding, so accommodating. If it is American to aim high and to respect one's own intelligence, then ninety percent of Hollywood films are un-American. If it is American to respect the creative instinct in writers and artists, then Hollywood, as a whole, is an un-American community, for the film industry has shown great contempt for the creative spirit and has encouraged instead the accommodating spirit. To the film industry, a work of art has seemed a property in need of butchery, not interpretation. We have not forgotten what an M-G-M executive said, a little more than a year ago, when his company was trying to silence the pen of Miss E. Arnot Robertson, the English critic, whose opinion of American films was that they were rather silly. The spokesman for M-G-M charged that Miss Robertson was not properly equipped to criticize pictures, because her opinions were "out of touch with those of the picture-going millions." His notion of a critic was somebody who felt the pulse of the millions, not somebody who watched the picture and examined his own conscience. We cite such a man for contempt—contempt of the millions whose intelligence he holds in such low regard.

It is easy to understand why Communists gravitate to Hollywood. They find there a favorable atmosphere, studios teeming with persons busy subverting the truth, and they receive there two of the things that make their life endurable—money and the daily proof that capitalist society has its silly side and its sour smell. But if the producers in Hollywood are sincere in their beliefs in America, they need not worry about Communists. All they need to do is make a good picture. A movie man who has made a good picture, a newspaper publisher who has put out a good issue, can walk through aisles of Communists on his way to work in the morning, and when he sits down the chair will feel solid under him and the room will not go round and round. Freedom of conscience is an elusive thing. Luckily, our Constitution writers, who felt no contempt for the people, pinned it down and wrote it into the great amendment that sustains us today, thus paying the individual the highest compliment it was possible to pay him. The free conscience in the responsible individual was awarded an Oscar in this land long before Hollywood started pinning medals on its idolized stars, and the free conscience won its Oscar not for any willingness to follow a script but for its tendency to depart from one.

I Spy

The games of little boys at play,
    I-Spy and Run-Sheep-Run,
Trouble the street the livelong day
    And all is for the fun.

And when the lads grow up in fame
    And make a subtler noise,
They plot and plan and play the game
    They played when they were boys.

In darkling street they seek and hide,
    The game grows wild and drunken;
They spy upon the other side,
    Keep secrets in a punkin.

So let us think on little boys
    And love-of-fire that lingers
On simple and remembered joys
    And how to burn the fingers.

The street grows dark, the night is hot,
    And so the game has trended.

Whether we know it, lads, or not,
    The game is nearly ended.

Run, sheep, run! Run wild and fast—
    A game to end the day with.
Look at the sky! A fire at last
    Too big for boys to play with!

Temple of Democracy

When the professors were dismissed from the University of Washington, the president remarked that allegiance to the Communist Party unfitted a teacher for the search for truth. The argument, it seemed to us, had a certain merit. To pursue truth, one should not be too deeply entrenched in any hole. It is best to have strong curiosity, weak affiliations. But although it's easy to dismiss a professor or make him sign an affidavit, it is not so easy to dismiss the issue of academic freedom, which persists on campuses as the smell of wintergreen oil persists in locker rooms. In this land, an ousted professor is not an island entire of itself; his death diminishes us all.

There is no question but that colleges and universities these days are under pressure from alumni and trustees to clean house and to provide dynamic instruction in the American way of life. Some institutions (notably Washington University and Olivet College) have already taken steps, others are uneasily going over their lists. Professors, meanwhile, adjust their neckties a little more conservatively in the morning, qualify their irregular remarks with a bit more care. The head of one small college announced the other day that his institution was through fooling around with fuzzy ideas and was going to buckle down and teach straight Americanism—which, from his description, sounded as simple as the manual of arms. At Cornell, an alumnus recently advocated that the university install a course in "Our Freedoms"—possibly a laudable idea but one that struck us as being full of dynamite. (The trouble here is with the word "our," which is too constricting and which would tend to associate a university with a national philosophy, as when the German universities felt the cold hand of the Ministry of Propaganda.) President Eisenhower has come out with a more solid suggestion, and has stated firmly that Columbia, while admiring one idea, will examine all ideas. He seems to us to have the best grasp of where the strength of America lies.

We on this magazine believe in the principle of hiring and firing on the basis of fitness, and we have no opinion as to the fitness or unfitness of the fired professors. We also believe that some of the firings in this country in the last eighteen months have resembled a political purge, rather than a dismissal for individual unfitness, and we think this is bad for everybody. Hollywood fired its writers in a block of ten. The University of Washington stood its professors up in a block of six, fired three for political wrongness, retained three on probation. Regardless of the fitness or unfitness of these men for their jobs, this is not good management; it is nervous management and it suggests pressure.

Indirectly, it abets Communism by making millions of highly fit Americans a little cautious, a little fearful of having naughty "thoughts," a little fearful of believing differently from the next man, a little worried about associating with a group or party or club.

A healthy university in a healthy democracy is a free society, in miniature. The pesky nature of democratic life is that it has no comfortable rigidity; it always hangs by a thread, never quite submits to consolidation or solidification, is always being challenged, always being defended. The seeming insubstantiality of this thread is a matter of concern and worry to persons who naturally would prefer a more robust support for the beloved structure. The thread is particularly worrisome, we think, to men of tidy habits and large affairs, who are accustomed to reinforce themselves at every possible turn and who want to do as much for their alma mater. But they do not always perceive that the elasticity of democracy is its strength—like the web of a spider, which bends but holds. The desire to give the whole thing greater rigidity and a more conventional set of fastenings is almost overwhelming in these times when the strain is great, and it makes professed lovers of liberty propose measures that show little real faith in liberty.

We believe with President Eisenhower that a university can best demonstrate freedom by not closing its doors to antithetical ideas. We believe that teachers should be fired not in blocks of three for political wrongness but in blocks of one for unfitness. A campus is unique. It is above and beyond government. It is on the highest plane of life. Those who live there know the smell of good air, and they always take pains to spell truth with a small "t." This is its secret strength and its contribution to the web of freedom; this is why the reading room of a college library is the very temple of democracy.

Death of the *Sun*

It surprised us not at all that when the *Sun* folded and the other papers wrote their obits and their tearful editorials about the foundering of a great ship that had held a true course, there was only one mention of the most distinguished *Sun* man of them all, Don Marquis. The fact that the *Sun* office was the place where the lower-case Archy, the bug with the soul of a poet, subsisted on stale paste and apple parings and performed his nightly labors on the typewriter keys proved not worth a passing notice. Ah, welladay! For many thousands of buyers of evening newspapers, there was one *Sun* man who outshone the Danas, the Munseys, the Arthur Brisbanes, the Richard Harding Davises, and the Frank Ward O'Malleys. For these people, the *Sun* died when Marquis left.

The death of the *Sun*, and the obsequies, reminded us of the death of Freddy the rat. Freddy was another celebrated inhabitant at the *Sun* office, a hated contemporary of Archy's. When Freddy died (following an encounter with a tarantula), they dropped him off the fire escape into an alley, with military honors. That is about what happens when a newspaper dies. Frank Munsey put it into words, and so did the tarantula.

The tarantula kept taunting Freddy. "Where I step," he said, "a weed dies." Munsey said it a little more elegantly. "The New York evening-newspaper field," he said in 1924, "is now in good shape through an elimination of an oversupply of evening newspapers. These evening newspapers have been eliminated as individual entities from New York journalism by myself alone." Where I step, a rag dies.

The first duty of a newspaper is to stay alive. And the most important single fact about any newspaper is that it differs from the next newspaper and is owned by a different man, or group of men. This fact (the fact of difference) transcends a newspaper's greatness, a newspaper's honesty, a newspaper's liveliness or any other quality. The health of the country deteriorates every time a newspaper dies of strangulation or is wiped out in a mercy killing. The solemn fact about the absorption of the *Sun* by Scripps-Howard is not that we lose a conservative paper, or an ancient paper, or an honest paper, or a funny paper, but that we lose a paper—one voice in the choir.

The recent episode of the broadcasts in Grand Central caused us to examine the newspapers in this town a bit more closely than usual, and we were not impressed by the violence of their emotions. The papers vigorously covered the story of the New York Central and its precedent-establishing racket in the Terminal; they played it for what it was worth, took pictures, and published full accounts of the goings on. But we

detected a peculiar absence of any sense of private con-
viction, one way or another. Brave as bulls in matters
concerning politics and corruption, the papers often
appear to be meek as lambs or playful as rabbits when
they approach any subject that is even remotely asso-
ciated with advertising and the deep-running streams
of revenue. For this reason, if for no other, it is doubly
important that we have many newspapers, many own-
ers, not a few.

And speaking of revenue, the final statement of the
Sun's publisher was written in such expensive lan-
guage as almost to explain the demise of his sheet.
Mr. Dewart said, "Mounting costs of production, unac-
companied by commensurate increases in advertising
revenue, have made some such course inevitable." That
kind of prose takes a heap of newsprint, plenty of type-
setting. Archy could have said it quicker, and cheaper.

The Thud of Ideas

Americans are willing to go to enormous trouble
and expense defending their principles with arms,
very little trouble and expense advocating them with
words. Temperamentally we are ready to die for cer-
tain principles (or, in the case of overripe adults, send
youngsters to die), but we show little inclination to ad-
vertise the reasons for the dying. Some critics say that
a self-governing, democratic people don't know what
they believe; but that is nonsense. It is simply that
a democratic people, who are also an impatient and
restless people, feel no strong urge to define what they
instinctively comprehend. Also, they do not delegate
to government the power to speak for the individual.
The disinclination to propagandize is characteristic.
Thirty-six billions for a military program, a thin buck
for a voice clarifying our aims and beliefs. Many peo-
ple now think, and we agree with them, that if we
are to compete successfully with the throaty call of
the Communist heartland—a call as brassy as that
of a tenting evangelist—we shall have to develop a bit
of a whistle of our own. We already have the Soviet
voice at a disadvantage, and we should exploit it. The
Russians limit themselves to spreading what they

call the Truth and to jamming the sounds that come from the other direction. They cannot disseminate information, because information would too often embarrass their Truth. We can do much better. We can, and should, spread the material an American reads each morning in his paper—news, definitions, letters to the editor, texts, credos, reports, recipes, aims and intentions. We must reach and astonish with our kind of reporting the millions who hear almost nothing of that sort and who hardly know it exists. We can safely leave Truth to the Kremlin, and can broadcast instead the splendid fact of difference of opinion, the thud of ideas in collision.

The Russian charge about us, which deliberately misleads many millions of people, should be met with a greatly expanded United States Department of Correction, Amplification, and Abuse. Misinformation, even when it is not deliberate, is at the bottom of much human misery. We recall the recent ordeal of George Kuscinkas, the fifty-six-year-old delivery man who pushed his handcart thirteen miles, far into the Bronx, because his employer had written "23rd Street" so that it looked like "234th Street." This was pure carelessness. But think of the journeys that are being made by those in the world who are pushing a heavy handcart in an impossible direction under misapprehensions of one sort and another!

We saw a piece in the paper the other day by a historian who had decided that freedom was shot because frontiers were disappearing. Freedom, he reasoned, can't survive in the congested conditions of a non-pioneering civilization. If there were anything to this theory, it would be the worst news of the week. We think the historian underestimates the vitality of the free spirit in the individual and exaggerates the role of geography. An iron curtain almost but not quite impenetrable is as challenging a frontier as a forest of virgin timber. Besides, it is perfectly apparent that freedom resides comfortably in areas of great congestion. We walked through such a street this morning.

Somehow the letters-to-the-editor page, strange and wonderful as it always is, is one of the chief adornments of the society we love and seek to clarify for the world. The privilege of writing to the editor is basic; the product is the hot dish of scrambled eggs that is America. Take the *Times* the other morning: a resounding letter headed "Awareness of Issues Asked," a student appeal to protect forest preserves ("Let this long and difficult fight be a lesson . . ."), an indignant attack by a Gaines Dog Research man on the superstition that dog days are associated with hydrophobia, a thoughtful essay on world government, and finally a blast from a reader in Monroe, New York: "It just so happens that I attempted to transplant three plants [of orange milkweed] recently and they all had long, horizontal roots." Such a page, together with the *Times*' sense of duty in publishing it, suggests an abiding normalcy in democratic behavior and thought, and gives the reassurance that neither Korea nor the volume of the Russian voice can unsettle this land whose citizens' torments and hopes, big and little, are aired daily in the press, this land whose roots are both long and horizontal.

Not Conforming to Facts

New words seem to be one of the by-products of crisis. Senator Taft has been dubbed "reexaminist" by Secretary Acheson. Mr. Stassen has dubbed himself "freedomist." The new words are almost as unbearable as the state of affairs they arise from. The North Koreans are, in the language of General Wu, "liberationists." Those who oppose them are "aggressors" or "imperialists." Wu himself might be described as a derivationist, or copycat.

We agree with Taft that our foreign policy should be reexamined. Being on Taft's side in this argument gives us a queasy feeling but does not permanently disable us. Foreign policy should be examined every hour on the hour, just as should every delicate plant or animal or child on which one's hopes are pinned. It seems to us that United States foreign policy is correct in its direction and its analysis, but every time we reexamine it, we find it lacking in showmanship and in scope.

The strategy of freedom leans heavily on Point 4 [a foreign aid program so named because it was the fourth foreign policy objective mentioned by President Harry Truman in his inaugural address], which was announced as a "big, bold" program of development and aid to backward areas. So far, Point 4 hasn't been big and it hasn't been bold. A pamphlet written by String-fellow Barr and just published makes this criticism with great clarity. Pamphlets and quick books on world salvation are another curious by-product of critical times, and we recommend Mr. Barr's little book as an exercise in reexamination. Without attempting to pass judgment on his broad-scale solution (creation under the United Nations of a World Development Authority), we agree with him that this country shows a too com-fortable tendency to underestimate the problem. Here is a reexaminist who is modest and thoughtful and who believes that we must convince our luckless and un-happy friends around the globe that there is something in our society more nourishing than the A-bomb.

No one can predict the turn of military events, but almost anybody can accurately predict one thing: Pov-erty and fear will continue to grip most of the people of the world for some time to come. United States policy is to strengthen the free nations and build our defenses. It is a correct policy and we should go at it relentlessly and fast. We should also remember that while we talk of "containment," the Soviets talk of "liberation." While Mr. Stassen rechristens us "freedomists," the Soviets dub their new puppet the "Central People's Govern-ment of the People's Republic of China" and millions of Red Chinese, although winded from saying the name of their own country, get a hazy idea that something wonderful has been done for them. Russia will always be able to trim us in the use of language, since she doesn't feel obliged to make it conform to facts. In order to compete successfully, we shall have to trim Russia in performance. The United Nations is the agency we have accepted for the job; Point 4 is one of the elements in the strategy. To keep it small and timid might be a very big mistake.

Murder of *La Prensa*

La Prensa was a conservative Buenos Aires newspaper that became entangled in a labor union and political squabble with Juan Perón, the former president of Argentina.

The influence of the crime investigation has been pervasive, particularly the influence of Senator Tobey's little accusatory lectures, which in retrospect seem to us a questionable form of fact-finding. Questionable or not, they set a pattern in the mind. We had occasion to call up a fellow at the U.N. the other morning, while the hearing was in progress, to ask him about the *Prensa* business, and in the course of our talk he remarked, "The Subcommission on Freedom of Information is dormant." "Well, wake it up!" we were about to shout, and then remembered that we weren't a senator, and our friend wasn't a witness, and the fierce religious light of television wasn't falling upon our conversation.

The murder of a newspaper is a lot like the murder of a person; it is apt to lead to further bloodshed in an attempt to destroy the evidence. Mr. Perón strangled *La Prensa* and was seen with the sash cord in his hand. All over the world, newspapers and magazines just happened to catch him in the act. So he is now taking the next step: he is knocking the witnesses over the head, in order to get *them* out of the way. Argentine customs authorities were instructed last week to seize certain newspapers and periodicals, so the dictator might be spared the embarrassment of having the Argentine public read about his crime. Thus does murder breed murder.

The closing of *La Prensa* is reminiscent of other slayings, in the not distant past, when other dictators, now dead, were busy silencing the free press. We had to fight a war over it, and that, too, is memorable. Even the terminology has a familiar sound—the use of the word "light" for the word "darkness." Dictators always create a language of their own. Mr. Perón, appearing recently at a conference of twenty-one American republics, called for a program to make the Western Hemisphere "a beacon of peace in a world of darkness." We prefer Webster's Dictionary in these crises; pending restoration of *La Prensa*, we shall refer to Mr. Perón's country as Darkest Argentina, and we would like to see it thus named whenever it is mentioned in the American press (now banned by him), as a continuing protest against these abominable deeds.

The *Prensa* affair stirs against the recurrent question: How can the United Nations shake off its impotency and show strength? The free world is rocked by the suppression of an independent newspaper and does not readily accept the explanation that it is a "domestic" matter. There is nothing domestic about the death of a newspaper. To kill off a newspaper is aggression. It is as menacing as to move an army across a border. If the Subcommission on Freedom of Information is dormant, then let the new Peace Observation Commission wake up and take *La Prensa* as its first assignment. What better observatory is there, if one is looking for evil stars, than a padlocked newspaper whose editor is being sought for arrest because he wrote a statement expressing his side of the case?

The U.N. has on its books a declaration of human rights, but it has no machinery for regulating human conduct. It cannot demand that the member nations perform the duties that underlie these rights, it cannot insist that member nations accept the responsibilities that would make these rights a reality. In short, it can watch *La Prensa* die and it can take notes, but it cannot bring the killer to account. The U.N., furthermore, does not impose any moral conditions of membership. The nations that were admitted in 1945, of which Darkest Argentina was one, were accepted by reason of their having been on the winning side in a world war—as silly a way of organizing a club as any we ever heard of. Right now, the U.N. weighs the advantage of having Russia at its conference table against the alternative advantage of having a set of basic principles on which members are agreed. It can't have both. But it won't have strength until it has principles—the first principle being a free press. The U.N. has behind it a strong world sentiment that seeks action in behalf of free principles. The time will come, soon or late, when this sentiment will dominate all other emotions and when the U.N. will decide to overhaul its charter and create a constitutional system of rights and duties, as a substitute for a mere working arrangement with Russia and her buddies. Then, if a nation wants to enjoy the pleasures and advantages of membership, it will have to fulfill the qualifications for membership. And the first of these shall be a free press, and no fooling.

Discredit of Others

We doubt that there ever was a time in this country when so many people were trying to discredit so many other people. About a year ago, we started to compile a handbook of defamation, showing who was disemboweling whom in America, but the list soon got too big for us and we abandoned the project as both unwieldy and unlovely. Discreditation has become a national sickness, for which no cure has so far been found, and there is a strong likelihood that we will all wake some morning to learn that in the whole land there is not one decent man. Vilification, condemnation, revelation—these supply a huge part of the columns of the papers, and the story of life in the United States dissolves into a novel of perfidy, rascality, iniquity, and misbehavior. The writing of this lurid tale commands more and more of the time of the citizens. And there is a living in this type of work, beyond any doubt. Pegler, who candidly disavows democracy, supports himself quite nicely by a daily variation on his theme of personal iniquity and stupidity, and by his affirmation that those whose ideas differ from his own are dangerous to have about. At this moment, we don't know who is readying the 1953 Smearbook, to carry on where Mortimer and Lait left off, but a man can be reasonably sure these days that such a book is in process. All these things give one pause and make the scene ominous in a way the facts do not support. Lately, the preoccupation of the electorate with Senator Nixon's finances almost completely obscured the bright, the heartening fact that in General Eisenhower and Governor Stevenson the country has a pair of candidates who have seldom been matched for distinction, for ability, and for probity, and that no matter which gets the job, we can thank our lucky stars as well as our secret booths.

In doubtful, doubting days, national morality tends to slip and slide toward a condition in which the test of a man's honor is his zeal for discovering dishonor in another. This is always a bad fix, never worse than today. It creates a shaky structure and accentuates the basic trouble. Nobody ever acquired strength by publishing somebody else's weakness, and to look for strength in that quarter is to grab at shadows. We hope and pray that our country, after November's results have settled the immediate dust, will perceive the gravity of her indisposition and take a corrective.

The ABC of Security

Said Mr. A to Mr. B,
"I doubt the loyalty of C."

Said Mr. B to Mr. A,
"I'm shocked and stunned by what you say;
We'd better check on him today,
And since you've brought up Mr. C,
I feel that I must mention D.
I rather doubt *his* loyalty."

Said Mr. F to Mr G,
"G, have you ever noticed B?
What do you make of his loyalty?"

Said Mr. G to Mr. F,
"Lower your voice—people aren't deaf!
I wouldn't want you quoting me,
But sure, I've always noticed B."

Said Mr. C to Mr. A,
"I saw a funny thing today;
At least, it seemed quite odd to *me*.

I saw F whispering with G
And I just caught the name of B."

"No, really?" answered A to C.
"Well, anyway—I don't know B.
I guess it's just as well for me."

And so the subtle poison spread
Until there rose a Mr. Zed.
The lightning played around his head.
"My fellow-countrymen," he said,
"The past, as you'll observe, is dead,
The alphabet's discredited;
You can't trust teachers now to teach,
You can't trust ministers to preach,
And it has been my special labor
To prove that none can trust his neighbor
In fact, it's amply clear to see
There's no one you can trust but me.
And by a happy turn of fate
I've come to purify the state.
My methods will be swift and strong
Against the crime of thinking wrong.
I know the cure for heresy
And you can leave it all to me.
Leave everything to me!" he said.

"Hurrah!" they cried. "Hurrah for Zed!"

FCC Background Noise

The Federal Communications Commission is playing with a scheme by which FM radio stations would provide "background music and weather and news reports" for stores, restaurants, streetcars, and buses. The Commission welcomes comment. Our comment should perhaps be directed to the clients—particularly to bus and streetcar companies, whose audiences are in attendance not from free choice but from necessity. Our comment is that there are always a few people (in stores, in restaurants, in streetcars, in buses) who prefer to receive their news from internal sources far removed from those of the Associated Press, who like to appraise the weather by staring down at the snow or up at the stars, and to whom the most acceptable background music for any occasion is the music of the spheres, privately recorded. The natural rights of such persons, hinted at in the Constitution, seem important to us, and we would recommend that the F.C.C. and all FM clients take such rights into consideration in deciding whether to bring news to captive audiences. This country is on the verge of getting news-drunk anyway; a democracy cannot survive merely by being well informed, it must also be contemplative, and wise. We believe news should be readily available to all who seek it, but should never be imposed on any who are engaged in digging it out for themselves or who need sleep.

One Hour to Think

President Eisenhower made it clear recently that he intended to reorganize his life so as to have one hour per day in which to think. He said he needed at least half an hour in the morning and half an hour at night to collect his thoughts. We applaud the move. One trouble of being a leader of thought in America is that it leaves no time for thinking, and currently the duties of president are so heavy that they pretty well carry a man through the day without his having to think at all, except in the most triggerish sort of fashion. As for ourself, of whom we can speak more knowingly than of Mr. Eisenhower, we have always attempted to organize our day so that we never had anything in particular to do, in the slim hope that if only we were idle, perhaps we might grow thoughtful. It has not worked. Thought is a by-product neither of perfect idleness nor of great activity but is an accidental sprout that appears unexpectedly on the vine of one's daily routine and that can be cultivated if one catches it soon enough and tends it with some kindliness and patience. Some of the most articulate and impressive persons we've known have not had a thought in their lives, or, rather, have never allowed one to develop naturally but have forced all for quick bloom. Most people, it would appear, hate to think and go to extremes to avoid it. The motion-picture houses we ourself have haunted in the devotional hours of our afternoons, to escape the ordeal of thought, if piled one atop the other, would dwarf Olympus.

It's quite possible that the Presidency of the United States has become an impossible job for one man, and that we need two men—an Acting President, to answer questions, make decisions, attend meetings, and listen to reports and gossip, and a Passive President, who merely watches, reflects on it, and finally, if a thought occurs to him, gives the country the benefit of it. Ideally, the two Presidents should be combined in a single individual, as they were in Lincoln, who had the stature and the temperament to be both active and passive. Not every elected leader is so well endowed by nature. Golf is not passivity, it is merely relief, and if the score is bad, it isn't even that. At any rate, there is much to think about, and we agree with Mr. Eisenhower—the days seem nowhere near long enough.

We don't know how the President organizes his "thought periods," his half-hour lozenges of pure cerebration. If he needs topics, we can supply a few. Liberty. Unity. Tranquility. Fertility. The rain and the wind. The light in the sky. The old, old look. Unity alone is good for a full half hour these days. The free nations are rattling around in what remains of their world like beads in a box. They await stringing. Instead of trying to string all together, we are mostly stringing each other along. In revolutionary times such as these, the United States should show forth clearly in a revolutionary light, as its history and its character entitle it to do, making of its democratic principles a world religion greater in impact than the religion of Communism. This cannot be achieved by the negative role of being anti-Communist; it can work only in a positive air of internal health and wide-ranging sympathy and concern for others. Democracy is harder to explain and harder to propound than Communism because it is subtler. Its devotees tend to take it for granted. There is every evidence, though, that we should not take it for granted, or assume that it is well understood or generally approved.

Bedfellows

I am lying here in my private sick bay on the east side of town between Second and Third avenues, watching starlings from the vantage point of bed. Three Democrats are in bed with me: Harry Truman (in a stale copy of the *Times*), Adlai Stevenson (in *Harper's*), and Dean Acheson (in a book called *A Democrat Looks at His Party*). I take Democrats to bed with me for lack of a dachshund, although as a matter of fact on occasions like this I am almost certain to be visited by the ghost of Fred, my dash-hound everlasting, dead these many years. In life, Fred always attended the sick, climbing right into bed with the patient like some lecherous old physician, and making a bad situation worse. All this dark morning I have reluctantly entertained him upon the rumpled blanket, felt his oppressive weight, and heard his fraudulent report. He was an uncomfortable bedmate when alive; death has worked little improvement—I still feel crowded, still wonder why I put up with his natural rudeness and his pretensions.

The only thing I used to find agreeable about him in bed was his smell, which for some reason was nonirritating to my nose and evocative to my mind, somewhat in the way that a sudden whiff of the cow barn or of bone meal on a lawn in springtime carries sensations of the richness of earth and of experience. Fred's aroma has not deserted him; it wafts over me now, as though I had just removed the stopper from a vial of cheap perfume. His aroma has not deserted the last collar he wore, either. I ran across this great, studded strap not long ago when I was rummaging in a cabinet. I raised it cautiously toward my nose, fearing a quill stab from his last porcupine. The collar was extremely high—had lost hardly ten percent of its potency. Fred was sold to me for a dachshund, but I was in a buying mood and would have bought the puppy if the storekeeper had said he was an Irish Wolfschmidt. He was only a few weeks old when I closed the deal, and he was in real trouble. In no time at all, his troubles cleared up and mine began. Thirteen years later he died, and by rights my troubles should have cleared up. But I can't say they have. Here I am, seven years after his death, still sharing a fever bed with him and, what is infinitely more burdensome, still feeling the compulsion to write about him. I sometimes suspect that subconsciously I'm trying to revenge myself by turning him to account, and thus recompensing myself for the time and money he cost me.

He was red and low-posted and long-bodied like a dachshund, and when you glanced casually at him he certainly gave the quick impression of being a dachshund. But if you went at him with a tape measure, and forced him onto scales, the dachshund theory collapsed.

The papers that came with him were produced hurriedly and in an illicit atmosphere in a back room of the pet shop, and are most unconvincing. However, I have no reason to unsettle the Kennel Club; the fraud, if indeed it was a fraud, was ended in 1948, at the time of his death. So much of his life was given to shady practices, it is only fitting that his pedigree should have been (as I believe it was) a forgery.

I have been languishing here, looking out at the lovely branches of the plane tree in the sky above our city back yard. Only starlings and house sparrows are in view at this season, but soon other birds will show up. (Why, by the way, doesn't the *Times* publish an "Arrival of Birds" column, similar to its famous "Arrival of Buyers"?) Fred was a window gazer and bird watcher, particularly during his later years, when hardened arteries slowed him up and made it necessary for him to substitute sedentary pleasures for active sport. I think of him as he used to look on our bed in Maine—an old four-poster, too high from the floor for him to reach unassisted. Whenever the bed was occupied during the daylight hours, whether because one of us was sick or was napping, Fred would appear in the doorway and enter without knocking. On his big gray face would be a look of quiet amusement (at having caught somebody in bed during the daytime) coupled with his usual look of fake respectability. Whoever occupied the bed would reach down, seize him by the loose folds of his thick neck, and haul him painfully up. He dreaded this maneuver, and so did the occupant of the bed. There was far too much dead weight involved for anybody's comfort. But Fred was always willing to put up with being hoisted in order to gain the happy heights, as, indeed, he was willing to put up with far greater discomforts— such as a mouthful of porcupine quills—when there was some prize at the end.

Once up, he settled into his pose of bird-watching, propped luxuriously against a pillow, as close as he could get to the window, his great soft brown eyes alight with expectation and scientific knowledge. He seemed never to tire of his work. He watched steadily and managed to give the impression that he was a secret agent of the Department of Justice. Spotting a flicker or a starling on the wing, he would turn and make a quick report.

"I just saw an eagle go by," he would say. "It was carrying a baby."

This was not precisely a lie. Fred was like a child in many ways, and sought always to blow things up to proportions that satisfied his imagination and his love of adventure. He was the Cecil B. deMille of dogs. He was also a zealot, and I have just been reminded of him by a quote from one of the Democrats sharing my bed—Acheson quoting Brandeis. "The greatest dangers to liberty," said Mr. Brandeis, "lurk in insidious encroachment by men of zeal, well-meaning but without understanding." Fred saw in every bird, every squirrel, every housefly, every rat, every skunk, every porcupine, a security risk and a present danger to his republic. He had a dossier on almost every living creature, as well as on several inanimate objects, including my son's football.

Although birds fascinated him, his real hope as he watched the big shade trees outside the window was that a red squirrel would show up. When he sighted a squirrel, Fred would straighten up from his pillow, tense his frame, and then, in a moment or two, begin to tremble. The knuckles of his big forelegs, unstable from old age, would seem to go into spasm, and he would sit there with his eyes glued on the squirrel and his front legs alternately collapsing under him and bearing his weight again.

I find it difficult to convey the peculiar character of this ignoble old vigilante, my late and sometimes lamented companion. What was there about him so different from the many other dogs I've owned that he keeps recurring and does not, in fact, seem really dead at all? My wife used to claim that Fred was deeply devoted to me, and in a certain sense he was, but his was the devotion of an opportunist. He knew that on the farm I took the overall view and travelled pluckily from one trouble spot to the next. He dearly loved this type of work. It was not his habit to tag along faithfully behind me, as a collie might, giving moral support and sometimes real support. He ran a trouble-shooting business of his own and was usually at the scene ahead of me, compounding the trouble and shooting in the air. The word "faithful" is an adjective I simply never thought of in connection with Fred. He differed from most dogs in that he tended to knock down, rather than build up, the master's ego. Once he had outgrown the capers of puppyhood, he never again caressed me or anybody else during his life. The only time he was ever discovered in an attitude that suggested affection was when I was in the driver's seat of our car and he would lay his heavy head on my right knee. This, I soon perceived, was not affection, it was nausea. Drooling always followed, and the whole thing was extremely inconvenient, because the weight of his head made me press too hard on the accelerator.

Fred devoted his life to deflating me and succeeded admirably. His attachment to our establishment, though untinged with affection, was strong nevertheless, and vibrant. It was simply that he found in our persons, in our activities, the sort of complex, disorderly society that fired his imagination and satisfied his need for tumult and his quest for truth. After he had subdued six or seven porcupines, we realized that his private war against porcupines was an expensive bore, so we took to tying him, making him fast to any tree or wheel or post or log that was at hand, to keep him from sneaking off into the woods. I think of him as always at the end of some outsize piece of rope. Fred's disgust at these confinements was great, but he improved his time, nonetheless, in a thousand small diversions. He never just lay and rested. Within the range of his tether, he continued to explore, dissect, botanize, conduct post-mortems, excavate, experiment, expropriate, savor, masticate, regurgitate. He had no contemplative life, but he held as a steady gleam the belief that under the commonplace stone and behind the unlikely piece of driftwood lay the stuff of high adventure and the opportunity to save the nation.

But to return to my other bedfellows, these quick Democrats. They are big, solid men, every one of them, and they have been busy writing and speaking, and sniffing out the truth. I did not deliberately pack my counterpane with members of a single political faith; they converged on me by the slick device of getting into print. All three turn up saying things that interest me, so I make bed space for them.

Mr. Truman, reminiscing in a recent issue of the *Times*, says the press sold out in 1948 to "the special interests," was ninety percent hostile to his candidacy, distorted facts, caused his low popularity rating at that period, and tried to prevent him from reaching the people with his message in the campaign. This bold, implausible statement engages my fancy because it is a half-truth, and all half-truths excite me. An attractive half-truth in bed with a man can disturb him as deeply as a cracker crumb. Being a second-string member of the press myself, and working, as I do, for the special interests, I tend to think there is a large dollop of pure irascibility in Mr. Truman's gloomy report. In 1948, Mr. Truman made a spirited whistle-stop trip and worked five times as hard as his rival. The "Republican-controlled press and radio" reported practically everything he said, and also gave vent to frequent horselaughs in their editorials and commentaries. Millions of studious, worried Americans heard and read what he said; then they checked it against the editorials; then they walked silently into the voting booths and returned him to office. Then they listened to Kaltenborn. Then they listened to Truman doing Kaltenborn. The criticism of the opposition in 1948 was neither a bad thing nor a destructive thing. It was healthy and (in our sort of society) necessary. Without the press, radio, and TV, President Truman couldn't have got through to the people in anything like the volume he achieved. Some of the published news was distorted, but distortion is inherent in partisan journalism, the same as it is in political rallies. I have yet to see a piece of writing, political or nonpolitical, that doesn't have a slant. All writing slants the way a writer leans, and no man is born perpendicular, although many men are born upright. The beauty of the American free press is that the slants and the twists and the distortions come from so many directions, and the special interests are so numerous, the reader must sift and sort and check and countercheck in order to find out what the score is. This he does. It is only when a press gets its twist from a single source, as in the case of government-controlled press systems, that the reader is licked.

Democrats do a lot of bellyaching about the press being preponderantly Republican, which it is. But they don't do the one thing that could correct the situation; they don't go into the publishing business. Democrats say they haven't got that kind of money, but I'm afraid they haven't got that kind of temperament or, perhaps, nerve.

Adlai Stevenson takes a view of criticism almost opposite to Harry Truman's. Writing in *Harper's*, Stevenson says, "... I very well know that in many minds 'criticism' has today become an ugly word. It has become almost *lése majesté*. It conjures up pictures of insidious radicals hacking away at the very foundations of the American way of life. It suggests nonconformity and nonconformity suggests disloyalty and disloyalty suggests treason, and before we know where we are, this process has all but identified the critic with the saboteur and turned political criticism into an un-American activity instead of democracy's greatest safeguard."

The above interests me because I agree with it and everyone is fascinated by what he agrees with. Especially when he is sick in bed.

Mr. Acheson, in his passionately partisan yet temperate book, writes at some length about the loyalty-security procedures that were started under the Democrats in 1947 and have modified our lives ever since. This theme interests me because I believe, with the author, that security declines as security machinery expands. The machinery calls for a secret police. At first, this device is used solely to protect us from unsuitable servants in sensitive positions. Then it broadens rapidly and permeates nonsensitive areas, and, finally, business and industry. It is in the portfolios of the secret police that nonconformity makes the subtle change into disloyalty. A secret-police system first unsettles, then desiccates, then calcifies a free society. I think the recent loyalty investigation of the press by the Eastland subcommittee was a disquieting event. It seemed to assume for Congress the right to poke about in newspaper offices and instruct the management as to which employees were O.K. and which were not. That sort of procedure opens wonderfully attractive vistas to legislators. If it becomes an accepted practice, it will lead to great abuses. Under extreme conditions, it could destroy the free press.

The loyalty theme also relates to Fred, who presses ever more heavily against me this morning. Fred was intensely loyal to himself, as every strong individualist must be. He held unshakable convictions, like Harry Truman. He was absolutely sure that he was in possession of the truth. Because he was loyal to himself, I found his eccentricities supportable. Actually, he contributed greatly to the general health and security of the household. Nothing has been quite the same since he departed. His views were largely of a dissenting nature. Yet in tearing us apart he somehow held us together. In obstructing, he strengthened us. In criticizing, he informed. In his rich, aromatic heresy, he nourished our faith. He was also a plain damned nuisance, I must not forget that.

The matter of "faith" has been in the papers again lately. President Eisenhower (I will now move over and welcome a Republican into bed, along with my other visitors) has come out for prayer and has emphasized that most Americans are motivated (as they surely are) by religious faith. The *Herald Tribune* headed the story, "PRESIDENT SAYS PRAYER IS PART OF DEMOCRACY." The implication in such a pronouncement, emanating from the seat of government, is that religious faith is a condition, or even a precondition, of the democratic life. This is just wrong. A President should pray whenever and wherever he feels like it (most Presidents have prayed hard and long, and some of them in desperation and in agony), but I don't think a President should advertise prayer. That is a different thing. Democracy, if I understand it at all, is a society in which the unbeliever feels undisturbed and at home. If there were only half a dozen unbelievers in America, their well-being would be a test of our democracy, their tranquility would be its proof. The repeated suggestion by the present administration that religious faith is a precondition of the American way of life is disturbing to me and, I am willing to bet, to a good many other citizens. President Eisenhower spoke of the tremendous favorable mail he received in response to his inaugural prayer in 1953. What he perhaps did not realize is that the persons who felt fidgety or disquieted about the matter were not likely to write in about it, lest they appear irreverent, irreligious, unfaithful, or even un-American. I remember the prayer very well. I didn't mind it, although I have never been able to pray electronically and doubt that I ever will be. Still, I was able to perceive that the President was sincere and was doing what came naturally, and anybody who is acting in a natural way is all right by me. I believe that our political leaders should live by faith and should, by deeds and sometimes by prayer, demonstrate faith, but I doubt that they should advocate faith, if only because such advocacy renders a few people uncomfortable. The concern of a democracy is that no honest man shall feel uncomfortable, I don't care who he is, or how nutty he is.

I hope that Belief never is made to appear mandatory. One of our founders, in 1787, said, "Even the diseases of the people should be represented." Those were strange, noble words, and they have endured. They were on television yesterday. I distrust the slightest hint of a standard for political rectitude, knowing that it will open the way for persons in authority to set arbitrary standards of human behavior. Fred was an unbeliever. He worshiped no personal God, no Supreme Being. He certainly did not worship me. If he had suddenly taken to worshiping me, I think I would have felt as queer as God must have felt the other day when a minister in California, pronouncing the invocation for a meeting of Democrats, said, "We believe

Adlai Stevenson to be Thy choice for President of the
United States. Amen."

I respected this quirk in Fred, this inability to con-
form to conventional canine standards of religious feel-
ing. And in the miniature democracy that was, and is,
our household he lived undisturbed and at peace with
his conscience. I hope my country will never become an
uncomfortable place for the unbeliever, as it could eas-
ily become if prayer was made one of the requirements
of the accredited citizen. My wife, a spiritual but not a
prayerful woman, read Mr. Eisenhower's call to prayer
in the *Tribune* and said something I shall never forget.
"Maybe it's all right," she said. "But for the first time
in my life I'm beginning to feel like an outsider in my
own land."

Democracy is itself a religious faith. For some it
comes close to being the only formal religion they have.
And so when I see the first faint shadow of orthodoxy
sweep across the sky, feel the first cold whiff of its
blinding fog steal in from sea, I tremble all over, as
though I had just seen an eagle go by, carrying a baby.

Anyway, it's pleasant here in bed with all these
friendly Democrats and Republicans, every one of them
a dedicated man, with all these magazine and newspa-
per clippings, with Fred, watching the starlings against
the wintry sky, and the prospect of another Presiden-
tial year, with all its passions and its distortions and
its dissents and its excesses and special interests. Fred
died from a life of excesses, and I don't mind if I do,

too. I love to read all these words—most of them sober, thoughtful words—from the steadily growing book of democracy; Acheson on security, Truman on the press, Eisenhower on faith, Stevenson on criticism, all writing away like sixty, all working to improve and save and maintain in good repair what was so marvelously constructed to begin with. This is the real thing. This is bedlam in bed. As Mr. Stevenson puts it: ". . . no civilization has ever had so haunting a sense of an ultimate order of goodness and rationality which can be known and achieved." It makes me eager to rise and meet the new day, as Fred used to rise to his, with the complete conviction that through vigilance and good works all porcupines, all cats, all skunks, all squirrels, all houseflies, all footballs, all evil birds in the sky could be successfully brought to account and the scene made safe and pleasant for the sensible individual— namely, him. However distorted was his crazy vision of the beautiful world, however perverse his scheme for establishing an order of goodness by murdering every creature that seemed to him bad, I had to hand him this: he really worked at it.

P.S. (June 1962). This piece about prayer and about Fred drew a heavy mail when it appeared—heavy for me, anyway. (I call six letters a heavy mail.) Some of the letters were from persons who felt as I did about the advocacy of prayer but who had been reluctant to say anything about it. And there were other letters from readers who complained that my delineation of

Fred's character (half vigilante, half dissenter) was contradictory, or at least fuzzy. I guess there is some justification for this complaint: the thing didn't come out as clear as I would have liked, but nothing I write ever does.

In the 1960 Presidential campaign, faith and prayer took a back seat and the big question was whether the White House could be occupied by a Catholic or whether that would be just too much. Again the voters studied the *Racing Form*, the *Wall Street Journal*, the *Christian Science Monitor*; they sifted the winds that blew through the Republican-controlled press; they gazed into television's crystal ball; they went to church and asked guidance; and finally they came up with the opinion that a Catholic can be President. It was a memorable time, a photo finish, and a healthful exercise generally.

The McCarthy era, so lately dead, has been followed by the Birch Society era (eras are growing shorter and shorter in America—some of them seem to last only a few days), and again we find ourselves with a group of people that proposes to establish a standard for political rectitude, again we have vigilantes busy compiling lists and deciding who is anti-Communist and who fails in that regard. Now in 1962, conservatism is the big, new correct thing, and the term "liberal" is a term of opprobrium. In the newspaper that arrives on my breakfast table every morning, liberals are usually referred to as "so-called" liberals, the implication being that they are probably something a whole lot worse than the name "liberal" would indicate, something really shady. The Birchers, luckily, are not in as good a position to create sensational newspaper headlines as was Senator McCarthy, who, because he was chairman of a Senate committee, managed to turn page one into a gibbet, and hung a new fellow each day, with the help of a press that sometimes seemed to me unnecessarily cooperative in donating its space for the celebration of those grim rites.

Prayer broke into the news again with the Supreme Court's decision in the New York school prayer case. From the violence of the reaction you would have thought the Court was in the business of stifling America's religious life and that the country was going to the dogs. But I think the Court again heard clearly the simple theme that ennobles our Constitution: that no one shall be made to feel uncomfortable or unsafe because of nonconformity. New York State, with the best intentions in the world, created a moment of gentle orthodoxy in public school life, and here and there a child was left out in the cold, bearing the stigma of being different. It is this one child that our Constitution is concerned about—his tranquility, his health, his safety, his conscience. What a kindly old document it is, and how brightly it shines, through interpretation after interpretation!

One day last fall I wandered down through the orchard and into the woods to pay a call at Fred's grave.

The trees were bare; wild apples hung shamelessly from the grapevine that long ago took over the tree. The old dump, which is no longer used and which goes out of sight during the leafy months, lay exposed and candid—rusted pots and tin cans and sundries. The briers had lost some of their effectiveness, the air was good, and the little dingle, usually so mean and inconsiderable, seemed to have acquired stature. Fred's headstone, ordinarily in collapse, was bolt upright, and I wondered whether he had quieted down at last. I felt uneasy suddenly, as the quick do sometimes feel when in the presence of the dead, and my uneasiness went to my bladder. Instead of laying a wreath, I watered an alder and came away.

This grave is the only grave I visit with any regularity—in fact, it is the only grave I visit at all. I have relatives lying in cemeteries here and there around the country, but I do not feel any urge to return to them, and it strikes me as odd that I should return to the place where an old dog lies in a shabby bit of woodland next to a private dump. Besides being an easy trip (one for which I need make no preparation) it is a natural journey—I really go down there to see what's doing. (Fred himself used to scout the place every day when he was alive.) I do not experience grief when I am down there, nor do I pay tribute to the dead. I feel a sort of overall sadness that has nothing to do with the grave or its occupant. Often I feel extremely well in that rough cemetery, and sometimes flush a partridge. But I feel sadness at All Last Things, too, which is probably a purely selfish, or turned-in, emotion—sorrow not at my dog's death but at my own, which hasn't even occurred yet but which saddens me just to think about in such pleasant surroundings.

Khrushchev and I (A Study in Similarities)

Until I happened to read a description of him in the paper recently, I never realized how much Chairman Khrushchev and I are alike. This fellow and myself, it turns out, are like as two peas. The patterns of our lives are almost indistinguishable, one from the other. I suppose the best way to illustrate this striking resemblance is to take up the points of similarity, one by one, as they appear in the news story, which I have here on my desk. Khrushchev, the story says, is a "devoted family man." Well, now! Could any phrase more perfectly describe me? Since my marriage in 1929, I have spent countless hours with my family and have performed innumerable small acts of devotion, such as shaking down the clinical thermometer and accidentally striking it against the edge of our solid porcelain washbasin. My devotion is too well known to need emphasis. In fact, the phrase that pops into people's heads when they think of me is "devoted family man." Few husbands, either in America or in the Soviet Union, have hung around the house, day in and day out, and never gone anywhere, as consistently as I have and over a longer period of time, and with more devotion. Sometimes it isn't so much devotion as it is simple curiosity—the fun of seeing what's going to happen next in a household like mine. But that's all right, too, and I wouldn't be surprised if some of the Chairman's so-called devotion was simple curiosity. Any husband who loses interest in the drama of family life, as it unfolds, isn't worth his salt.

Khrushchev, the article says, "enjoys walking in the woods with his five grandchildren." Here, I have to admit, there is a difference between us, but it is slight: I have only three grandchildren, and one of them can't walk in the woods, because he was only born on June 24 last and hasn't managed to get onto his feet yet. But he has been making some good tries, and when he does walk, the woods are what he will head for if he is anything like his brother Steven and his sister Martha and, of course, me. We all love the woods. Not even Ed Wynn loves the woods better than my grandchildren and me. We walk in them at every opportunity, stumbling along happily, tripping over windfalls, sniffing valerian, and annoying the jay. We note where the deer has lain under the wild apple, and we watch the red squirrel shucking spruce buds. The hours I have spent walking in the woods with my grandchildren have been happy ones, and I hope Nikita has had such good times in his own queer Russian way, in those strange Russian woods with all the bears. One bright cold morning last winter, I took my grandchildren into the woods through deep snow, to see the place where we were cutting firewood for our kitchen stove (I probably shouldn't tell this, because I imagine Khrushchev's wife has a modern gas or electric stove in her house, and not an old wood-burner, like us Americans). But anyway, Martha fell down seventeen times, and Steven disappeared into a clump of young skunk spruces, and I had all I could do to round up the children and get them safely out of the woods, once they had become separated that way. They're young, that's the main trouble. If anything, they love the woods too well. The newspaper story says Khrushchev leads a "very busy" life. So do I. I can't quite figure out why I am so busy all the time; it seems silly and it is against my principles. But I know one thing: a man can't keep livestock and sit around all day on his tail. For example, I have just designed and built a cow trap, for taking a Hereford cow by surprise. This job alone has kept me on the go from morning till night for two weeks, as I am only fairly good at constructing things and the trap still has a few bugs in it. Before I became embroiled in building the cow trap, I was busy with two Bantam hens, one of them on ten eggs in an apple box, the other on thirteen eggs in a nail keg. This kept me occupied ("very busy") for three weeks. It was rewarding work, though, and the little hens did the lion's share of it, in the old sweet barn in the still watches of the night. And before that it was haying. And before haying it was babysitting—while my daughter-in-law was in the hospital having John. And right in the middle of everything I went to the hospital myself, where, of course, I became busier than ever. Never spent a more active nine days. I don't know how it is in Russia, but the work they cut out for you in an American hospital is almost beyond belief. One night, after an exhausting day with the barium sulphate crowd, I had to sit up till three in the morning editing a brochure that my doctor handed me—something he had written to raise money for the place. Believe me, I sank down into the covers tired *that* night. Like Khrushchev, I'm just a bundle of activity, sick or well.

Khrushchev's wife, it says here, is a "teacher." My wife happens to be a teacher, too. She doesn't teach school, she teaches writers to remove the slight imperfections that mysteriously creep into American manuscripts, try though the writer will. She has been teaching this for thirty-four years. Laid end to end, the imperfections she has taught writers to remove from manuscripts would reach from Minsk to Coon Rapids. I am well aware that in Russia manuscripts do not have imperfections, but they do in this country, and we just have to make the best of it. At any rate, both Mrs. Khrushchev and my wife are teachers, and that is the main point, showing the uncanny similarity between Khrushchev and me.

Khrushchev, it turns out, has a daughter who is a "biologist." Well, for goodness' sake! I have a *step*-daughter who is a biologist. She took her Ph.D. at Yale and heads the science department at the Moravian

Seminary for Girls. Talk about your two peas! Inciden-
tally, this same stepdaughter has three children, and
although they are not technically my grandchildren,
nevertheless they go walking in the woods with me, so
that brings the woods total to five, roughly speaking,
and increases the amazing similarity.

Khrushchev's son is an "engineer," it says. Guess
what college my son graduated from! By now you'll
think I'm pulling your leg, but it's a fact he gradu-
ated from the Massachusetts Institute of Technology.
He hasn't launched a rocket yet, but he has launched
many a boat, and when I last saw him he held the moon
in his hand—or was it a spherical compass?

"The few hours Khrushchev can spare for rest and
relaxation he usually spends with his family." There I
am again. I hope when Khrushchev, seeking rest and
relaxation, lies down on the couch in the bosom of his
family, he doesn't find that a dog has got there first and
that he is lying on the dog. That's my biggest trouble in
relaxing—the damn dog. To him a couch is a finer in-
vention than a satellite, and I tend to agree with him.
Anyway, in the hours I can spare for rest, it's family life
for me. Once in a great while I sneak down to the shore
and mess around in boats, getting away from the fam-
ily for a little while, but every man does that, I guess.
Probably even Khrushchev, devoted family man that
he is, goes off by himself once in a great while, to get
people out of his hair.

Already you can see how remarkably alike the two

of us are, but you haven't heard half of it. During vacations and on Sundays, it says, Khrushchev "goes hunting." That's where I go, too. It doesn't say what Khrushchev hunts, and I won't hazard a guess. As for me, I hunt the croquet ball in the perennial border. Sometimes I hunt the flea. I hunt the pullet egg in the raspberry patch. I hunt the rat. I hunt the hedgehog. I hunt my wife's reading glasses. (They are in the pocket of her housecoat, where any crafty hunter knows they would be.) Nimrods from away back, Khrush and I.

Khrushchev has been an "avid reader since childhood." There I am again. I have read avidly since childhood. Can't remember many of the titles, but I read the books. Not only do I read avidly, I read slowly and painfully, word by word, like a child reading. So my total of books is small compared to most people's total, probably smaller than the Chairman's total. Yet we're both avid readers.

And now listen to this: "Mr. Khrushchev is the friend of scientists, writers, and artists." That is exactly my situation, or predicament. Not all scientists, writers, and artists count me their friend, but I do feel very friendly toward Writer Frank Sullivan, Artist Mary Petty, Scientist Joseph T. Wearn, Pretty Writer Maeve Brennan, Artist Caroline Angell, Young Writer John Updike—the list is much too long to set down on paper. Being the friend of writers, artists, and scientists has its tense moments, but on the whole it has been a good life, and I have no regrets. I think probably it's more fun being a friend of writers and artists in America than in the Soviet Union, because you don't know in advance what they're up to. It's such fun wondering what they're going to say next.

Another point of similarity: Mr. Khrushchev, according to the news story, "devotes a great deal of his attention to American-Soviet relations." So do I. It's what I am doing right this minute. I am trying to use the extraordinary similarity between the Chairman and me to prove that an opportunity exists for improving relations. Once, years ago, I even wrote a book about the relations between nations. I was a trifle upset at the time, and the book was rather dreamy and uninformed, but it was good-spirited and it tackled such questions as whether the moon should be represented on the Security Council, and I still think that what I said was essentially sound, although I'm not sure the timing was right. Be that as it may, I'm a devoted advocate of better relations between nations—Khrush and I both. I don't think the nations are going about it the right way, but that's another story.

"No matter how busy Khrushchev is," the article says, "he always finds time to meet Americans and converse with them frankly on contemporary world problems." In this respect, he is the spit and image of me. Take yesterday. I was busy writing and an American walked boldly into the room where I was trying to finish a piece I started more than a year ago and would have finished months ago except for interruptions of one sort and another, and what did I do? I shoved everything aside and talked to this American on contemporary world problems. It turned out he knew almost nothing about them, and I've never known much about them, God knows, except what I see with my own eyes, but we kicked it around anyway. I have never been so busy that I wouldn't meet Americans, or they me. Hell, they drive right into my driveway, stop the car, get out, and start talking about contemporary problems even though I've never laid eyes on them before. I don't have the protection Khrushchev has. My dog welcomes any American, day or night, and who am I to let a dog outdo me in simple courtesy?

Mr. Khrushchev, the story goes on, "has a thorough knowledge of agriculture and a concern for the individual worker." Gee whizz, it's me all over again. I have learned so much about agriculture that I have devised a way to water a cow (with calf at side) in the barn cellar without ever going down the stairs. I'm too old to climb down stairs carrying a twelve-quart pail of water. I tie a halter rope to the bail of the pail (I use a clove hitch) and lower the pail through a hatch in the main floor. I do this after dark, when the cow is thirsty and other people aren't around. Only one person ever caught me at it—my granddaughter. She was enchanted. Ellsworth, my cow, knows about the routine, and she and her calf rise to their feet and walk over to the pail, and she drinks, in great long, audible sips, with the light from my flashlight making a sort of spot on cow and pail. Seen from directly above, at a distance of only four or five feet, it is a lovely sight, almost like being in church—the great head and horns, the bail relaxed, the rope slack, the inquisitive little calf attracted by the religious light, wanting to know, and sniffing the edge of the pail timidly. It is, as I say, a lovely, peaceable moment for me, as well as a tribute to my knowledge of agriculture. As for the individual worker whom Khrushchev is concerned about, he is much in my mind, too. His name is Henry. [Henry Allen, White's indispensable helper on the Maine farm.]

Well, that about winds up the list of points of similarity. It is perhaps worth noting that Khrushchev and I are not wholly alike—we have our points of difference, too. He weighs 195, I weigh 132. He has lost more hair than I have. I have never struck the moon, even in anger. I have never jammed the air. I have never advocated peace and friendship; my hopes are pinned on law and order, the gradual extension of representative government, the eventual federation of the free, and the end of political chaos caused by the rigidity of sovereignty. I have never said I would bury America, or received a twenty-one-gun salute for having said it. I feel, in fact, that America should not be buried. (I like the *Times* in the morning and the moon at night.) But these are minor differences, easily reconciled by revolution, war, death, or a change of climate. The big thing is that both Khrushchev and I like to walk in the woods with our grandchildren. I wonder if he has noticed how dark the woods have grown lately, the shadows deeper and deeper, the jay silent. I wish the woods were more the way they used to be. I wish they were the way they could be.

Unity

After "Unity" was published, Utah's senator Frank E. Moss gained unanimous consent for its inclusion in the *Congressional Record*. "Mr. President," he said, "once in a long while someone writes on a matter of consuming national importance with such penetration and clarity that the emerging analysis carries an undeniable ring of truth and authority in every line. . . . The article is essential reading, in my opinion, for both those who believe in the status quo and those who would start marching, with or without a clear purpose . . . so that it might be discussed up and down the land by people of all ages and political faiths." The piece ran in the *Congressional Record* on June 29, 1960.

In 1899, the year I was born, a peace conference was held at The Hague. I don't remember how it came out, but there have been two memorable wars since then, and I am now sixty, and peace parleys, some of them tackling the subject of disarmament, have been held at intervals all my life. At this writing, five nations of the East and five of the West are studying disarmament, hopeful of achieving peace. When last heard from, they were deadlocked, which is the natural condition of nations engaged in arms negotiations. The Soviet Union has suggested that they "start all over again."

The West has a real genius for doing approximately what the East wants it to do. We go to Paris and sit in stunned surprise while Khrushchev bangs a cat against a wall. We go to Geneva and listen solemnly while Russia presents herself as the author of total disarmament and peace. We hasten to the Security Council room at the United Nations and earnestly defend ourselves against a charge that we have "aggressed." We join England for Princess Margaret's wedding, and next day we separate from England again, to return our trust to last-minute diplomatic conformity. We use the word "peace" the way the East likes to see it used—in the last paragraph of the President's formal speeches, and preceded by the adjectives "just" and "lasting," as if peace were some sort of precious stone that, once discovered, would put an end to trouble for all time. I am beginning to tire of running the East's errands and dropping into the East's traps, and I wish I could set off on a different journey, under good auspices.

Senator McClellan, in a speech at Valley Forge quite a while back, said that "the only hope for freedom's survival" was moral, spiritual, political, economic, and military strength. (He should have added "intellectual strength.") Happily, freedom, if there is such an entity, is well fixed for four out of five of the Senator's ingredients. Freedom has great moral strength; this is its principal advantage over Communism. Freedom has the strength of spirit. Freedom is strong economically— in the United States and in many other capitalist countries. It is strong in military power. But it is sadly lacking in political strength, because it does not enjoy the benefits of political unity and, unlike Communism, does not lay a course for it. Two free nations, though they may pull together in a crisis, are almost as far apart diplomatically as a free nation and a Communist nation. The two free nations are obliged to conduct their affairs as though they were fencing with each other, as indeed they are, with parries and thrusts, occasionally unmasking to smile and shake hands and test each other for popularity and good will. After the recent events in Paris, and the bruises of that night, it is not at all certain that the West should indulge itself longer in the pleasures of perfect political disunity. [A May 14, 1960, Paris Summit, arranged between Khrushchev and Eisenhower, had collapsed after a U.S. spy plane was shot down over Russia just thirteen days before.]

Soviet arms, terrible as they are, seem less fearsome to me than the Soviet's dedication to its political faith, which includes the clear goal of political unity. Russia openly proclaims her intention of Communizing the world and announces that she is on the march. Not all her cronies present the face of unity—Mao's China, Tito's Yugoslavia, Gomulka's Poland—but at least the idea of unity is implicit in the religion of Communism. Must we in the West leave all the marching to our opponent? I hope not. Not until free men get up in the morning with the feeling that they, too, are on the march will the danger to Western society begin to subside. But marching is futile unless there is a destination, and the West's destination is fuzzy. Perhaps I should merely say that it is not clear to me. I do not think it is discernible in the utterances of our statesmen.

Lately, I have been browsing among the books and published speeches of some of the candidates for Presidency. Here are some of the themes against which the contestants knock their heads: disarmament, nuclear testing, foreign aid, civil liberties, a farm program, trade expansion, payola, race relations, admission of Red China to the U.N., peace with honor, peace with justice, peace with safety, peace under the rule of law, peace through *détente*, better housing, better education, the missile gap, a strengthened defense, the exploration of space. I have read Kennedy, Bowles, Nixon, Stevenson, Rockefeller, and others. They speak of new principles for a new age, but for the most part I find old principles for a time that is past. Most of the special matters they discuss are pressing, but taken singly, or added together, they do not point in a steady direction, they do not name a destination that gets me up in the morning to pull on my marching boots. Once in a while I try a little march on my own, stepping out briskly toward a reputable hill, but when I do I feel that I am alone, and that I am on a treadmill. The way things are now, we could all march for the rest of our days and still not advance perceptibly. This is not true of the Soviets. They know perfectly well where they want to be. Lately, it has seemed that they might get there.

Life Magazine, I see, has raised the question of the free world's destiny with a series of pieces on "National Purpose." The title of the series is revealing. America's purpose, everyone's purpose in the West, is still painted in the national frame. When we aid a friend, it is "foreign" aid. And when the aided country emerges, it gains "independence," thus adding one more sovereign political unit to the ever-growing list of destiny seekers. When we establish a military base in some indispensable location outside our borders, we call it a base on "foreign" soil, and so it is. The U-2 plane incident disclosed an American pilot taking off from an American nook in Turkey and heading for an American nook in Norway. This famous flight illustrated the queer condition we and our Western associates are compelled to face—a world grown so small that other people's airfields are essential to our own safety, and ours to theirs, yet a world that has made no progress in bringing free men together in a political community and under a common roof. The West's only roof these days is the wild sky, with its flights, its overflights, and the boom of broken barriers. Our scientists long ago broke all known boundaries, yet the rest of us work sedulously to maintain them, in our pursuits, in our prayers, in our minds, and in our constitutions. We dwell in a house one wall of which has been removed, all the while pretending that we are still protected against the wind and the rain.

Most people think of peace as a state of Nothing Bad Happening, or Nothing Much Happening. Yet if peace is to overtake us and make us the gift of serenity and well-being, it will have to be the state of Something Good Happening. What is this good thing? I think it is the evolution of community, community slowly and surely invested with the robes of government by the consent of the governed. We cannot conceivably achieve a peaceful life merely by relaxing the tensions of sovereign nations; there is an unending supply of them. We may gain a breather by relaxing a tension here and there, but I think it is a fallacy that a mere easement, or diplomacy triumphant, can ever be the whole base for peace. You could relax every last tension tonight and wake up tomorrow morning with all the makings of a war, all the familiar promise of trouble.

A popular belief these days is that the clue to peace is in disarmament. Pick a statesman of any stature in any nation and he will almost certainly tell you that a reduction in arms is the gateway of peace. Unfortunately, disarmament doesn't have much to do with peace. I sometimes wish it had, it enjoys such an excellent reputation and commands such a lot of attention. Keeping itself strong is always a nation's first concern whenever arms are up for discussion, and disarmament is simply one of the devices by which a nation tries to increase its strength relative to the strength of others. On this naked earth, a nation that approaches disarmament as though it were a humanitarian ideal is either suffering from delusions or deliberately planning a deception.

Chairman Khrushchev recently asked, "Is there any . . . way which would remove the threat of war without prejudicing the interests of states?" and then answered his own question: "We see it in the general and complete disarmament of states." Now, even if one were to believe that Mr. Khrushchev is averse to prejudicing the interests of states, one might still wonder whether any state relieved of its weapons was thereby relieved of the threat of war. I am afraid that blaming armaments for war is like blaming fever for disease. Khrushchev's total-disarmament bid was made for the same reason he makes other bids; namely, to advance the cause of international Communism. Total disarmament would not leave anyone free of the threat of war, it would simply leave everyone temporarily without the help of arms in the event of war. Disarmament talks divert our gaze from the root of the matter, which is not the control of weapons, or weapons themselves, but the creation of machinery for the solution of the problems that give rise to the use of weapons.

Disarmament, I think, is a mirage. I don't mean it is indistinct, or delusive, I mean it isn't there. Every ship, every plane could be scrapped, every stockpile destroyed, every soldier mustered out, and if the original reasons for holding arms were still present, the world would not have been disarmed. Arms would simply be in a momentary state of suspension, preparatory to new and greater arms. The eyes of all of us are fixed on a shape we seem to see up ahead—a vision of a world relaxed, orderly, secure, friendly. Disarmament looks good because it sounds good, but unhappily one does not get rid of disorder by getting rid of munitions, and disarmament is not solid land containing a harbor, it is an illusion caused by political phenomena, just as a mirage is an illusion caused by atmospheric phenomena, a land mass that doesn't exist.

Weapons are worrisome and expensive; they make everyone edgy. But weapons are not and never have been the cause of trouble. The only weapon in this decade that is intrinsically harmful is the nuclear weapon during its test period, and that is a new and separate problem, which must be dealt with separately. I think it can and will be dealt with, but although it is related to the balance of power, and therefore is capable of being used for national advantage, it carries a threat that is the same for all nations, Eastern and Western, atomic and non-atomic—the threat that the earth will eventually bear too great a residue of poison and will no longer support life. All nations know this, although some are reluctant to admit it. At any rate, a test ban, though full of danger for whoever signs it, has at least a reasonable chance of success, provided the nations signing it do not disarm. A nation signing an agreement to quit exploding nuclear weapons has a selfish interest in honoring the agreement. The debris from its tests falls on home ground as well as on enemy territory; it covers the earth like the dew. And although the nation might find many attractive reasons for breaking the agreement, the selfish reason would still be present, as a deterrent to violation. That is why we may profitably talk about stopping nuclear tests: national self-interest happens in this case to coincide with universal interest, and the whole business is simply a matter of human survival on a shaky planet. Usually, in negotiations, that isn't true. It isn't true of a disarmament agreement, which is no sooner signed than a thousand selfish reasons crop up for wanting to violate it.

We hold arms so that, in the event of another nation's breaking its word, we will have something to fall back on, something by which we can command respect, enforce our position, and have our way. Modern arms are complicated by their very destructiveness, their ability to turn and bite whoever unleashes them. That is why everyone is pleased by the prospect of disarming and why there is a great hue and cry raised against arms. And how are we to disarm? By signing a treaty. And what is a treaty? A treaty is a document that is generally regarded as so untrustworthy we feel we must hold arms in order to make sure we're not disadvantaged by its being broken. In other words, we are seriously proposing to sign an agreement to abandon the very thing we will need in the event that the agreement itself fails to stick. This seems a queer program to me.

In drawing up plans for disarming, the nations are making it clear that their distrust of one another and of treaties is as strong as ever. They're insisting that there be "controls"—they are called "adequate" controls—and that there be "inspection." President Eisenhower has suggested an "open sky" system. And everybody agrees that the treaty must be "enforceable"—some say by an international disarmament organization free of the veto and affiliated with the United Nations. As for control, there is no way to control any aspect of a sovereign nation's internal life. The U.N. designers sensibly bowed to this sticky fact when they installed the veto and provided that the internal affairs of a member should be nobody else's business. (The Hungarian revolt demonstrated how sad are the facts of international life.) It is possible to *influence* a sovereign nation, through public opinion and through pressures of one sort and another, but it's not possible to control it, short of domination by force. In the case of arms, which are among the most intimate of a nation's garments, and which a nation instinctively conceals from view, we do not even know at any given moment what we would be hoping to control the next moment, so speedy is the evolution of weapons and counter-weapons. National life is secret life. It has always been secret, and I think it is necessarily secret. To live openly, one must first have a framework of open living—a political framework very different from anything that now exists on the international level. A disarmament arrangement backed by controls and inspection is not such a framework, it is simply a veiled invitation to more and greater secrecy.

Can we inspect the Soviet Union? Can it inspect us? In this jungle world, inspection would be an attempt to license an international legion of Peeping Toms. I cannot believe that it would work. It would probably spawn a legion of counter-Toms, fellows to peep at the peepers. An "open sky" system in which the inspectors carried operator's licenses would itself be under surveillance of the open-sky system that all nations feel obliged to maintain at all times. And the open-sky system, although a new idea, has already been overtaken by events: the sovereign sky is no longer top-level—space hangs above it, from which the East and West are taking pictures of each other with flying cameras.

As for "enforcement," an arms pact is by its nature unenforceable. It would be enforceable only if there was an authority higher or more powerful than that of the parties involved in the deal. The principal characteristic of life on earth today is that no such authority exists. An international disarmament organization, created by treaty and representing the East and West and equipped with police powers, would not constitute such an authority. This does not mean that nations do not take their treaty obligations seriously; it simply means that no nation takes any obligation seriously if it begins to threaten the national safety or obstruct the national will. In the case of a disarmament "authority," any attempt to invoke it might easily result in a riot or a war. National arms would quickly resume their ascendancy over pooled arms, because national forces are responsive to the will of the nation, and this is a fluid, living thing; whereas international arms would be the servant of the sovereign powers and of a status quo—the conditions that prevailed on the day the treaty was signed. The Soviet Union wants this police force to be under the Security Council, where it would be subject to the vote—in short, a cop who would swing his club or fail to swing it according to the whim of one of the parties.

Many statesmen feel that weapons are in themselves evil and that they should be eliminated, as you would crush a snake. They feel that vast stores of arms create tension and threaten the peace by the mere fact of their existence. This is perfectly true. I doubt, though, whether the tension created by the existence of arms is as great as the tension if there were no arms, or too few arms. President Eisenhower has said that war in this day and age would yield "only a great emptiness." So, I think, would disarmament in this day and age. An arms race is a frightening thing, but eighty sovereign nations suddenly turning up without arms is truly terrifying. One may even presume that Russia came forward with the most sensational of the disarmament proposals—total disarmament in four years—just because it *is* terrifying. A dictator dearly loves a vacuum, and he dearly loves to rattle people. Disarmament in this day would increase, not diminish, the danger of war. Today's weapons are too destructive to use, so they stand poised and quiet; this is our strange climate, when arms are safer than no arms. If modern weapons make war unlikely, had we not better keep them until we have found the political means of making war unnecessary?

In a letter to Dag Hammarskjöld [a Swedish diplomat and economist, Dag Hjalmar Agne Carl Hammarskjöld was the second secretary-general of the United Nations, and forty-seven years old when appointed], Khrushchev said, "General and complete disarmament cannot result in advantage to any side." This is nonsense. The side that enjoys numerical superiority stands to gain by disarmament, the side that does not have any intention of remaining unarmed for more than a few minutes stands to gain, and the side that uses the lie as an instrument of national policy stands to gain. If disarmament carried no chance of advantage, Mr. Khrushchev would not be wasting his breath on it. He likes it because of its propaganda value and because it gives him a chance to oust us from our advanced military bases—which is the Soviet's precondition of an arms agreement.

Perhaps the most valuable clues to peace nowadays are to be found in the Soviet Union's own fears, and those are many. Russia's greatest fear, apparently, is that Western democracies will act in a united and constructive way. Russia is constantly on the alert to divide us and drive the wedge that we read about every day in the papers. Mr. Khrushchev's March visit to Paris was designed primarily to arouse France against West Germany. His conniptions at the summit and his vilification of President Eisenhower were designed to stir up irritation and allow him to threaten the countries that had accidently got involved in the spy-plane affair. If it's so very important to Russia that the West be a house divided against itself, then it should be equally important to the free nations that they stand together, not simply as old friends who have a common interest but as a going political concern. A successful attempt to open discussion on this subject has yet to be made, and the matter is seldom referred to in exact terms. The Western nations are still content to put their trust in what they know—techniques of diplomacy, of alliance, of collective security, of bargaining, of last-ditch solidarity. A few months ago, when the United States and Great Britain were faced with a decision about nuclear-test arrangements, [Prime Minister Harold] Macmillan had to duck over here at the eleventh hour for a quick talk. This kind of hasty tucking up should be unnecessary. It is appalling that at this late date the two great English-speaking nations, both equipped with atomic weapons, both desirous of presenting a solid front to the world, each wholly dependent on the other for survival and neither sure that it will survive, should have no political machinery for translating the wishes of their people and should be obliged to go philandering to gain a decision on some vital point. England and America in this fateful decade remind me of a fabulous two-headed sheep I encountered in a book by Laurie Lee: "It could sing harmoniously in a double voice and cross-question itself for hours."

While studying the words of the candidates, I watched for signs that any of them felt favorably disposed toward a more positive and orderly political structure for the West. The signs are there, but the words are thin, guarded, hesitant, as was to be expected. Few public men are willing to state the thing unconditionally and with enthusiasm. But here, for what they are worth, are a few hints, a few promising sprouts:

Adlai Stevenson: "Should we not at least attempt a political inventiveness which in some ways matches the horrific inventiveness of our scientists? . . . We do not pursue the general welfare. We pursue our separate national interests and hope that the selfish good of the parts will add up—against the witness of all social history—to the wider good of the whole. We do not urgently seek a world under law."

And again Mr. Stevenson: "A working cooperative Atlantic system would do more than enhance the basic strength of the West. It would demonstrate to other areas . . . methods by which political autonomy can be combined with supranational cooperation. In any case, the alternative is to see the centrifugal forces which are always at work between separate national entities pull us ever further apart. One thing is sure—we cannot deal with the Communist challenge divided and in disarray."

Vice-President Nixon: "The time has now come to take the initiative in . . . establishment of the rule of law in the world to replace the rule of force."

Senator [John F.] Kennedy: "With respect to the world outside, our purpose is not only to defend the integrity of this democratic society but also to help advance the cause of freedom and world law—the universal cause of a just and lasting peace."

And again Mr. Kennedy: "So far we have lacked the vision to present a comprehensive program for the development of a world commentary under law and we have lacked the courage to try small beginnings."

Nelson Rockefeller: "[The United States should seek] a political framework which someday may be comparable to the one we created for our own nation in the federation of states on a worldwide basis."

Chester Bowles: "The gradual growth of a framework of world law will depend on the vitality and success of the multilateral agencies we now have, and we should be vigorously pursuing our objectives through these agencies wherever possible."

The phrase "the rule of law," I have noticed, means different things to different men. Mr. Nixon's amplification of the remark quoted above indicated that he found the rule of law in a strengthened World Court, which I think is to confuse international law with supranational law. I'm not sure I know what Mr. Kennedy means by the rule of law. President Eisenhower sometimes uses the phrase and leaves the interpretation up to the listener.

Governor Stevenson goes as far as "a working cooperative Atlantic system" and "supranational cooperation." Governor Rockefeller comes right out with a federal principle and with a "political framework . . . comparable to the one we created for our nation."

Well, politicians are busy men. Primarily they are not paid to indulge in the pastime of shaping the world in an ideal mold, out of pure theory and pure reason; they are paid to get us through the day as best they can. A public servant has a thousand pressing obligations as well as a strong distaste for theoretical ideas that are bound to irritate voters. But I believe that if a public man speaks of the rule of law at all, he should stay with the subject long enough to say what he has in mind: Who are the authors of this law? Who are the enforcers? From whom do they derive their authority? What are the geographical conditions? What is the framework within which it lives? The simple truth is, we in the West have not yet attempted a political inventiveness, we do not seek a political framework, the centrifugal forces causing friendly nations to fly apart are still operating, we are in disarray, and "the rule of law" is a cloudy phrase in a closing paragraph, not a clear gleam in somebody's eye.

Perhaps this is not the proper time to explore the foundation of unity of the West. Many people would say that although the vision of a federal union of free democratic capitalist states is a pleasing prospect for dreamers, actual work on it would be too upsetting, would shake us at a ticklish time. We might become so absorbed in establishing order on a higher level that we'd lose what little order we now enjoy, and thus play into the hands of our enemies. Others would say that if the political unity of free powers were to become an accomplished fact, it would merely increase the challenge and the fury of the East. Others would argue that most people find unity repugnant; it spoils the fun.

These are all good arguments against trying to bring greater order into Western society. As an American citizen, though, I would welcome the stirrings of political union with the United Kingdom, with France, with Scandinavia, with all the Western European nations—with any nation, in fact, that could show a long, successful record of government by the consent of the governed. For I would feel that although I was being placed temporarily in a more dangerous position, I was nevertheless occupying higher ground, where the view was better. I would know my destination at last. If from the shambles of the summit there were to emerge the first positive thrust of Western unity, then the summit would, in my book, go down as a smashing success, not a bleak failure.

The Communists have a shape they pursue; they propose an Eastern union that will eventually erode the West and occupy the globe. In a day when imperialism is despised and languishing, they brazenly construct an empire. To do this they engage us in a Cold War. I believe this war would be easier to fight if we, too, could find a shape to pursue, a proposal to make. Let us pursue the shape of English liberty—what Santayana once described as "this slow cooperation of free men, this liberty in democracy." English liberty in a federal hall—there's a shape to conjure with! "Far from being neutralized by American dash and bravura," wrote Santayana, "or lost in the opposite instincts of so many alien races, it seems to be adopted at once in the most mixed circles and in the most novel predicaments." A federation of free states, with its national units undisturbed and its people elevated to a new and greater sovereignty, is a long way off, by anybody's guess; but if we could once settle on it among ourselves, and embrace it unashamedly, then we would begin to advance in a clear direction and enjoy the pleasures and disciplines of a political destination. Liberty is never out of bounds or off limits; it spreads wherever it can capture the imagination of men.

Speaking of engaging men's minds, this is another thing we seem willing to leave to the Russians. The figures on it are appalling. The authors that are circulated most widely today, in translation, are Marx, Lenin, and Stalin. Between 1948 and 1955, Lenin ran ahead of the Bible. I don't know where he stands today in relation to the Bible—he may have slipped a little— but I know where he stands in relation to John Adams, James Madison, Benjamin Franklin, Thomas Jefferson, and some of the other writers we like to think are stimulating to readers. He is out in front by a commanding lead—one that will be hard to overcome. We in America have no right even to brood about the unity of free men unless we are energetic enough to make our ideas available to those who are desperately seeking any idea at all. The Army fired a missile the other day and hit a target nine thousand miles away, but we've put very little time or money into launching our best missile—our ideas. We should flood the world with the good books that make men's hearts catch fire. We should not expect the man in the antipodes to travel to the corner of Forty-second Street and Fifth Avenue and search through the card catalogue.

These are the times of daily horror and daily fear. Men are now talking of digging holes in the ground for everybody, into which all can crawl. But I think men are not built like fiddler crabs. What we need in this awesome century is not a hole that goes down a few feet into the earth, but a clear working drawing of a structure that goes well up into the air. There have been such times before, but these are by far the gravest.

In the long debate on disarmament, I encountered

a statement that has proved memorable; it was in a piece in the *Times* magazine last October, by Salvador de Madariaga, who for a number of years watched disarmament from the League of Nations. Señor de Madariaga ended his article with an observation that should inform and enliven every free nation. "The trouble today," he wrote, "is that the Communist world understands unity but not liberty, while the free world understands liberty but not unity. Eventual victory may be won by the first of the two sides to achieve the synthesis of both liberty and unity."

I have never seen the matter stated more succinctly, nor have I ever read a prediction I felt such confidence in. President Eisenhower often talks of "peace with justice," but fails to supply a sketch. Diplomacy, treaties, national aspirations, peace parley hot, peace parley cold, good-will tours, secrecy, spying, foreign aid, foreign trade, foreign relations—these seem to be the only building blocks we are trustful of. From them justice cannot be expected to arise, although occasionally some benefits do come from them, more by good luck than by good management. Our national strategy goes something like this: Keep your chin up, keep your powder dry, be willing to negotiate, keep your friends happy, be popular, be strong, get to outer space, stall for time, justice is bound to come eventually, and the rule of law.

I doubt whether justice, which is the forerunner of peace, will ever be pulled out of a hat, as some suppose.

Justice will find a home where there is a synthesis of liberty and unity in a framework of government. And when justice appears on any scene, on any level of society, man's problems enjoy a sort of automatic solution, because they enjoy the means of solution. Unity is no mirage. It is the distant shore. I believe we should at least head for that good shore, though most of us will not touch it in this life.

Burdens of High Office

As they walked out of the Presidential office, Mr.
Kennedy took a white handkerchief from his pocket
and wiped the boy's nose.

—THE TIMES

A President's work is never done,
His burdens press from sun to sun:
A Berlin wall, a racial brew,
A tax-cut bill, a Madame Nhu.
One crisis ebbs, another flows—
    And here comes John with a runny nose.

A President must rise and dress,
See senators, and meet the press,
Be always bold, be sometimes wary,
Be kind to foreign dignitary,
And while he's fending off our foes
    Bend down and wipe a little boy's nose.

Freedom of Choice
(Letter to the *Weekly Packet*)

July 2, 1964

To the Editor of the *Packet*:

I believe freedom to be the opposite of what you seem to think it is. Personal liberty really arises from men's willingness to submit to restraints that protect the many from the whimsical conduct of the few.

I watched "freedom of choice" at work in the Nineteen Twenties, when brokerage houses were free to operate as they saw fit. What resulted was a financial crash that left millions of Americans without any choice at all, except the choice of whether to jump or not. Nowadays, thanks to market controls, we have a stable economy that allows us to breathe free.

Negroes came to this country because ship owners had freedom of choice, and the owners chose to bring black men here in chains. For the past hundred years the Negro, although "emancipated," has had little free choice. What the Civil Rights Law says, in effect, is that a businessman who runs a public place may not decide what fellow is a member of the public and what fellow isn't. That seems morally right to me. And I think the *Packet* enjoys personal liberty not because it is free to say anything it pleases but because it must abide by the laws of libel and of decency.

—E. B. White

Democracy Is Destructible
(Letter to the *Bangor Daily News*)

October 8, 1964

To The Editor:

Senator Goldwater has occasionally used the phrase "obviously guilty," referring to criminals. This is a very unsettling thing. Nobody is "obviously" guilty in this country—a man is innocent until the court decides otherwise. Goldwater appears to believe that it's more important to catch a criminal than to preserve the principle of search and seizure, which is a bedrock of our jurisprudence, safeguarding our homes.

The NEWS is my morning paper and I crack it every day with interest. Lately it has been of very special interest because of the heat and importance of this campaign. I've been reading the Goldwater books and studying the Goldwater record, as every citizen should do, and I find his fundamentalist philosophy both absorbing and alarming. He would have us return to the verities, which is fine by me. But the pattern of this journey back into our better selves closely parallels the classic pattern of authoritarianism and the police state: discrediting the court, intimidating the press (I can still hear those boos and catcalls when the press was mentioned in San Francisco [the 1964 Republican

National Convention was held in the Cow Palace]—a truly ugly sound), depicting the federal government as the enemy of the people, depicting social welfare as the contaminant in our lives, promising to use presidential power to end violence, arguing that the end justifies the means (catch the thief, never mind how), promising victory now in an age of delicate nuclear balance, slyly suggesting that those of opposite opinion are perhaps of questionable loyalty, and always insisting that freedom has gone down the drain.

Your correspondent William Buckley reminded us the other day, via Tocqueville, that democracy is destructible. It is, indeed. It can be destroyed by a single zealous man who holds aloft a freedom sign while quietly undermining all of freedom's cherished institutions.

—E. B. White

Margaret Chase Smith
(Letter to the Senator)

August 15, 1966

Dear Senator Smith:

I think the Dirksen amendment on voluntary prayer should be defeated. The Constitution is clear on the subject: there shall be no establishment of religion.

Any religious ceremony in a public school is an exercise in orthodoxy—the orthodoxy of the Christian faith, which is correct for most of us, unacceptable to some. In an atmosphere of "voluntary" prayer, pupils coming from homes where other faiths prevail will feel an embarrassment by their non-participation; in the eyes of their schoolmates they will be "queer" or "different" or "irreligious." Such a stigma for a child can be emotionally disturbing, and although we no longer hang and burn our infidels and our witches, a schoolchild who is left out in the cold during a prayer session suffers scars that are very real.

It should be the concern of our democracy that no child shall feel uncomfortable because of belief. This condition cannot be met if a schoolmaster is empowered to establish a standard of religious rectitude based on a particular form of worship.

Sincerely yours,
E. B. White

Carnegie Commission on Educational Television (Letter to Stephen White)

Stephen White, an acquaintance of White's, wrote from the Carnegie Commission on Educational Television, asking for suggestions. White's reply was included in the commission's report.

September 26, 1966

Dear Steve:

I have a grandson now named Steven White, and I'll bet he can swim faster and stay under longer than you can.

As for television, I doubt that I have any ideas or suggestions that would be worth putting on paper. Non-commercial TV should address itself to the idea of excellence, not the idea of acceptability—which is what keeps commercial TV from climbing the staircase. I think TV should be providing the visual counterpart of the literary essay, should arouse our dreams, satisfy our hunger for beauty, take us on journeys, enable us to participate in events, present great drama and music, explore the sea and the sky and the woods and the hills. It should be our Lyceum, our Chautauqua, our Minsky's, and our Camelot. It should restate and clarify the social dilemma and the political pickle. Once in a while it does, and you get a quick glimpse of its potential.

As you see, I have nothing specific to offer and am well supplied with platitudes, every one of them gilt-edged. But thanks for the chance.

Yrs,
E. B. White

Press Must Be Free
(Letter to the *Bangor Daily News*)

November 5, 1970

To The Editor:

I see that you are now using the phrase "radical liberal" to describe certain citizens who endanger the Republic. This package label, implying that there is no distinction between radical and liberal, is the invention of Vice-President Agnew, a very inventive fellow.

Labels are labels, and they always turn up around election time. I'd like to remind the NEWS that quite recently the Vice-President came up with a most peculiar suggestion. He suggested that certain members of the news media—commentators on TV, specifically—be scrutinized by "government personnel" to discover what "types" they were and to see whether they should be holding the jobs they were in. This suggestion, casting the shadow of government interference with the press, is perhaps the most radical suggestion I've heard advanced by a public figure in my entire life, and I'm 71.

I doubt that the *Bangor Daily News* wants its reporters and its editorial writers screened by government personnel.

There's only one kind of press that's any good—a

press free from any taint of government control. So if you're looking for a radical thinker these days, I suggest that you take a good long hard look at the Vice-President of the United States. His name is Spiro T. Agnew, and in a very soft voice he has raised the specter of government supervision of the news.

E. B. White

On Hope (Letter to Mr. Nadeau)

March 30, 1973

Dear Mr. Nadeau:

As long as there is one upright man, as long as there is one compassionate woman, the contagion may spread and the scene is not desolate. Hope is the thing that is left to us, in a bad time. I shall get up Sunday morning and wind the clock, as a contribution to order and steadfastness.

Sailors have an expression about the weather: they say, the weather is a great bluffer. I guess the same is true of our human society—things can look dark, then a break shows in the clouds, and all is changed, sometimes rather suddenly. It is quite obvious that the human race has made a queer mess of life on this planet. But as a people we probably harbor seeds of goodness that have lain for a long time, waiting to sprout when the conditions are right. Man's curiosity, his relentlessness, his inventiveness, his ingenuity have led him into deep trouble. We can only hope that these same traits will enable him to claw his way out.

Hang on to your hat. Hang on to your hope. And wind the clock, for tomorrow is another day.

Sincerely,
E. B. White

Don't Bet on It
(Letter to the *Bangor Daily News*)

March 27, 1975

To The Editor:

I agree with you that there is only one decent and responsible way to decide something—let the people speak and then count the votes. I hope we never abandon that cherished principle.

But we should not, on the other hand, ever assume (as your editorial "The People Speak" seems to assume) that the people, given a chance to vote, always come up with the best answer. Americans have a lot of common sense; they also make mistakes on occasion.

The millions and millions who voted Richard Nixon into office were doing their level best at the polls but they blew it just the same. There is no assurance that the people of Searsport haven't blown it, either, on the issue of nuclear power. They simply did their best, according to their lights. Let's hope they were right. But don't bet on it.

E. B. White

The Xerox Letters (Letter to the Editor of the *Ellsworth American*, and Follow-up)

January 1, 1976

To the Editor:

I think it might be useful to stop viewing fences for a moment and take a close look at *Esquire* magazine's new way of doing business. In February, *Esquire* will publish a long article by Harrison E. Salisbury, for which Mr. Salisbury will receive no payment from *Esquire* but will receive $40,000 from the Xerox Corporation—plus another $15,000 for expenses. This, it would seem to me, is not only a new idea in publishing, it charts a clear course for the erosion of the free press in America. Mr. Salisbury is a former associate editor of the *New York Times* and should know better. *Esquire* is a reputable sheet and should know better. But here we go—the Xerox–Salisbury–*Esquire* axis in full cry!

A news story about this amazing event in the December 14th issue of the *Times* begins: "Officials of *Esquire* magazine and of the Xerox Corporation report no adverse reactions, so far, to the announcement that *Esquire* will publish a 23-page article [about travels through America] in February 'sponsored' by Xerox." Herewith I am happy to turn in my adverse reaction even if it's the first one across the line.

Esquire, according to the *Times* story, attempts to justify its new payment system (get the money from a sponsor) by assuring us that Mr. Salisbury will not be tampered with by Xerox; his hand and his pen will be free. If Xerox likes what he writes about America, Xerox will run a "low keyed full-page ad preceding the article" and another ad at the end of it. From this advertising, *Esquire* stands to pick up $115,000, and Mr. Salisbury has already picked up $40,000, traveling, all expenses paid, through this once happy land. . . .

Apparently Mr. Salisbury had a momentary qualm about taking on the Xerox job. The *Times* reports him as saying, "At first I thought, gee whiz, should I do this?" But he quickly conquered his annoying doubts and remembered that big corporations had in the past been known to sponsor "cultural enterprises," such as opera. The emergence of a magazine reporter as a cultural enterprise is as stunning a sight as the emergence of a butterfly from a cocoon. Mr. Salisbury must have felt great, escaping from his confinement.

Well, it doesn't take a giant intellect to detect in all this the shadow of disaster. If magazines decide to farm out their writers to advertisers and accept the advertiser's payment to the writer and to the magazine, then the periodicals of this country will be far down the drain and will become so fuzzy as to be indistinguishable from the controlled press in other parts of the world.

E. B. White

Some weeks after his letter on the Xerox–*Esquire*–Salisbury arrangement was published, White received a letter of inquiry from W. B. Jones, director of communications operations at Xerox Corporation, outlining the ground rules of the corporation's sponsorship of the Salisbury piece and concluding, "With these ground rules, do you still see something sinister in the sponsorship? The question is put seriously, because if a writer of your achievement and insight—after considering the terms of the arrangement—still sees this kind of corporate sponsorship as leading the periodicals of this country toward the controlled press of other parts of the world, then we may well reconsider our plans to underwrite similar projects in the future." White's reply to W. B. Jones follows.

January 30, 1976

Dear Mr. [W. B.] Jones:

In extending my remarks on sponsorship, published in the *Ellsworth American*, I want to limit the discussion to the press—that is, to newspapers and magazines. I'll not speculate about television, as television is outside my experience and I have no ready opinion about sponsorship in that medium.

In your recent letter to me, you ask whether, having studied your ground rules for proper conduct in sponsoring a magazine piece, I still see something sinister in the sponsorship. Yes, I do. Sinister may not be the right word, but I see something ominous and

unhealthy when a corporation underwrites an article
in a magazine of general circulation. This is not,
essentially, the old familiar question of an advertiser
trying to influence editorial content; almost everyone
is acquainted with that common phenomenon.
Readers are aware that it is always present but
usually in a rather subdued or non-threatening form.
Xerox's sponsoring of a specific writer on a specific
occasion for a specific article is something quite
different. No one, as far as I know, accuses Xerox of
trying to influence editorial opinion. But many people
are wondering why a large corporation placed so much
money on a magazine piece, why the writer of the
piece was willing to get paid in so unusual a fashion,
and why *Esquire* was ready and willing to have
an outsider pick up the tab. These are reasonable
questions.

The press in our free country is reliable and useful
not because of its good character but because of its
great diversity. As long as there are many owners,
each pursuing his own brand of truth, we the people
have the opportunity to arrive at the truth and to
dwell in the light. The multiplicity of ownership is
crucial. It's only when there are few owners, or, as in
a government-controlled press, one owner, that the
truth becomes elusive and the light fails. For a citizen
in our free society, it is an enormous privilege and
a wonderful protection to have access to hundreds
of periodicals, each peddling its own belief. There is

safety in numbers: the papers expose each other's
follies and peccadillos, correct each other's mistakes,
and cancel out each other's biases. The reader is free
to range around in the whole editorial bouillabaisse
and explore it for the one clam that matters—the
truth.

When a large corporation or a rich individual
underwrites an article in a magazine, the picture
changes: the ownership of that magazine has been
diminished, the outline of the magazine has been
blurred. In the case of the Salisbury piece, it was
as though *Esquire* had gone on relief, was accepting
its first welfare payment, and was not its own man
anymore. The editor protests that he accepts full
responsibility for the text and that Xerox had nothing
to do with the whole business. But the fact remains
that, despite his full acceptance of responsibility,
he somehow did not get around to paying the bill.
This is unsettling and I think unhealthy. Whenever
money changes hands, something goes along with
it—an intangible something that varies with
the circumstances. It would be hard to resist the
suspicion that *Esquire* feels indebted to Xerox, that
Mr. Salisbury feels indebted to both, and that the
ownership, or sovereignty, of *Esquire* has been nibbled
all around the edges.

Sponsorship in the press is an invitation to
corruption and abuse. The temptations are great,
and there is an opportunist behind every bush.

A funded article is a tempting morsel for any
publication—particularly for one that is having a
hard time making ends meet. A funded assignment
is a tempting dish for a writer, who may pocket a
much larger fee than he is accustomed to getting.
And sponsorship is attractive to the sponsor himself,
who, for one reason or another, feels an urge to
penetrate the editorial columns after being so long
pent up in the advertising pages. These temptations
are real, and if the barriers were to be let down
I believe corruption and abuse would soon follow.
Not all corporations would approach subsidy in the
immaculate way Xerox did or in the same spirit
of benefaction. There are a thousand reasons for
someone's wishing to buy his way into print, many
of them unpalatable, all of them to some degree
self-serving. Buying and selling space in news
columns could become a serious disease of the press.
If it reached epidemic proportions, it could destroy
the press. I don't want IBM or the National Rifle
Association providing me with a funded spectacular
when I open my paper, I want to read what the editor
and the publisher have managed to dig up on their
own—and paid for out of the till. . . .

My affection for the free press in a democracy
goes back a long way. My love for it was my first
and greatest love. If I felt a shock at the news of
the Salisbury–Xerox–*Esquire* arrangement, it
was because the sponsorship principle seemed to

challenge and threaten everything I believe in: that the press must not only be free, it must be fiercely independent—to survive and to serve. Not all papers are fiercely independent, God knows, but there are always enough of them around to provide a core of integrity and an example that others feel obliged to steer by. The funded article is not in itself evil, but it is the beginning of evil and it is an invitation to evil. I hope the invitation will not again be extended, and, if extended, I hope it will be declined.

About a hundred and fifty years ago, Tocqueville wrote: "The journalists of the United States are generally in a very humble position, with a scanty education and a vulgar turn of mind." Today, we chuckle at this antique characterization. But about fifty years ago, when I was a young journalist, I had the good fortune to encounter an editor who fitted the description quite closely. Harold Ross, who founded the *New Yorker*, was deficient in education and had—at least to all outward appearances—a vulgar turn of mind. What he did possess, though, was the ferocity of independence. He was having a tough time finding money to keep his floundering little sheet alive, yet he was determined that neither money nor influence would ever corrupt his dream or deflower his text. His boiling point was so low as to be comical. The faintest suggestion of the shadow of advertising in his news and editorial columns would cause him to erupt. He would explode in anger, the building would reverberate with his wrath, and his terrible swift sword would go flashing up and down the corridors. For a young man, it was an impressive sight and a memorable one. Fifty years have not dimmed for me either the spectacle of Ross's ferocity or my own early convictions—which were identical with his. He has come to my mind often while I've been composing this reply to your inquiry.

I hope I've clarified by a little bit my feelings about the anatomy of the press and the dangers of sponsorship of articles. Thanks for giving me the chance to speak my piece.

Sincerely,

E. B. White

Mr. Jones wrote and thanked White for "telling me what I didn't want to hear." In May, another letter arrived from Jones saying that Xerox had decided not to underwrite any more articles in the press and was convinced it was "the right decision."

Reverses of Fortune

Our Misfortunes in Canada are enough to melt an
Heart of Stone. The Small Pox is ten times more
terrible than Britons, Canadians and Indians
together. . . . There has been Want, approaching to
Famine, as well as Pestilence. . . but these Reverses
of Fortune don't discourage me. It is natural to expect
them, and We ought to be prepared in our Minds for
greater Changes, and more melancholly Scenes still.

So wrote John Adams to Abigail, in one of his mercurial moments, June 26, 1776. We don't know how far into the future he was gazing, but if he were around today, celebrating our two-hundredth, he would not lack for melancholy scenes. As far as the eye can see in any direction, corruption and wrongdoing, our rivers and lakes poisoned, our flying machines arriving before the hour of their departure, our ozone layer threatened, our sea gasping for breath, our fish inedible, our national bird laying defective eggs, our economy inflated, our food adulterated, our children weaned on ugly plastic toys, our diversions stained with pornography and obscenity, violence everywhere, venery in Congress, cheating at West Point, the elms sick and dying, our youth barely able to read and write, the Postal Service buckling under the burden of the mails and terrified by gloom of night, our sources of energy depleted, our railroads in decline, our small farms disappearing, our small businesses driven against the wall by bureaucratic edicts, and our nuclear power plants hard at work on plans to evacuate the countryside the minute something goes wrong. It is indeed a melancholy scene.

There is one thing, though, that can be said for this beleaguered and beloved country—it is alive and busy. It was busy in Philadelphia in 1776, trying to get squared away on a sensible course; it is busy in New York and Chillicothe today, trying to straighten out its incredible mess. The word "patriotic" is commonly used for Adams and for those other early geniuses. Today, the word is out of favor. Patriotism is unfashionable, having picked up the taint of chauvinism, jingoism, and demagoguery. A man is not expected to love his country, lest he make an ass of himself. Yet our country, seen through the mists of smog, is curiously lovable, in somewhat the way an individual who has got himself into an unconscionable scrape often seems lovable—or at least deserving of support. What other country is so appalled by its own shortcomings, so eager to atone for its own bad conduct? What other country ever issued an invitation like the one on the statue in New York's harbor? Wrongdoing, debauchery, decadence, decline—these are no more apparent in America today than are the myriad attempts to correct them and the myriad devices for doing it. The elms may be dying, but someone has developed a chemical compound that can be injected into the base of the elm tree to inhibit the progress of the disease. The Hudson River may be loaded with polychlorinated biphenyls, but there is an organization whose whole purpose is to defend and restore the Hudson River. It isn't as powerful as General Electric, but it is there, and it even gets out a little newspaper. Our food is loaded with carcinogens, while lights burn all night in laboratories where people are probing the mysteries of cancer. Everywhere you look, at the desolation and the melancholy scene, you find somebody busy with an antidote to melancholy, a cure for disease, a correction for misconduct. Sometimes there seems almost too much duplication of good works and therapeutic enterprise; but at least it suggests great busyness—a tremendous desire to carry on, against odds that, in July of 1976, as in June of 1776, often seem insuperable.

> But these Reverses of Fortune don't discourage
> me. . . . It is an animating Cause, and brave Spirits
> are not subdued with Difficulties.

Let us, on this important day when the tall ships move up the poisoned river, take heart from good John Adams. We might even for a day assume the role of patriot, with neither apology nor shame. It would be pleasant if we could confront the future with confidence, it would be relaxing if we could pursue happiness without worrying about a bad fish. But we are stuck with our chemistry, our spraymongers, our raunchy and corrupt public servants, just as Adams was stuck with the Britons, the Canadians, the Indians, and the shadow of Small Pox. Let not the reverses discourage us—liberty is an animating Cause (and there's not much smallpox around, either). If the land does not unfold fair and serene before our eyes, neither is this a bad place to be. It is unquestionably a busy one. Bang the bell! Touch off the fuse! Send up the rocket! On to the next hundred years of melancholy scenes, splendid deeds, and urgent business!

Credits

HIGH AMBIGUITY
The New Yorker, January 28, 1928.
Every Day Is Saturday. New York: Harper & Bros., 1934.

DISSENTING SUPREME COURT JUSTICE
The New Yorker, June 22, 1929.

STATEMENT OF THE FOREIGN POLICY OF ONE CITIZEN OF
THE UNITED STATES
The Conning Tower. *New York Herald Tribune*, January 29,
1934.
Fox of Peapack and Other Poems. New York: Harper & Bros.,
1938.

DOWN WITH CAKE
The New Yorker, May 12, 1934.
Fox of Peapack and Other Poems. New York: Harper & Bros.,
1938.

CONTROLLED OPINION
The New Yorker, August 10, 1935.

FREEDOM OF THE AIR (AND THE RIGHT TO SILENCE . . .)
The New Yorker, February 1, 1936.

POLITICAL BENEFICIARIES
The New Yorker, March 7, 1936.

NOW . . . THE JUDICIARY
The New Yorker, March 13, 1937.

I SAY TO YOU, CHEERIO
The New Yorker, May 22, 1937.
Fox of Peapack and Other Poems. New York: Harper & Bros., 1938.

STANDARDS OF JOURNALISM
The New Yorker, January 22, 1938.

TOTAL MORAL RESISTANCE
The New Yorker, June 22, 1940.

FREEDOM
One Man's Meat column. *Harper's Magazine*, September 1940.
One Man's Meat. New York: Harper & Bros., 1942.
An E. B. White Reader. Ed. William W. Watt and Robert W. Bradford. New York: Harper and Row, 1966.

INTIMATIONS
One Man's Meat column. *Harper's Magazine*, February 1942 [written in December 1941].
One Man's Meat. New York: Harper & Bros., 1942.

TREASON, DEFINED (WHEN CONGRESS DELAYS AN ISSUE)
The New Yorker, August 22, 1942.

CRACKPOTS
The New Yorker, September 12, 1942.
Writings from The New Yorker*, 1925–1976*. Ed. Rebecca M. Dale. New York: HarperCollins, 1990.

THE MEANING OF DEMOCRACY
The New Yorker, July 3, 1943; repr. April 28, 2014.
The Wild Flag. Boston: Houghton Mifflin Co., 1946.

DEFINITION OF FASCISM
The New Yorker, August 7, 1943.

PREFACE TO *THE WILD FLAG*
The Wild Flag. Boston: Houghton Mifflin Co., 1946.

NO FOOLING
The New Yorker, December 9, 1944.

BILL OF HUMAN RIGHTS
The New Yorker, March 31, 1945.

RIGHT TO WORK
The New Yorker, June 23, 1945.

INTERNATIONAL JUSTICE SYSTEM
The New Yorker, October 20, 1945.
The Wild Flag. Boston: Houghton Mifflin Co., 1946.

PEARL HARBOR INVESTIGATION
The New Yorker, December 8, 1945.

INSTRUCTIONS TO A DELEGATE
The Wild Flag. Boston: Houghton Mifflin Co., 1946.

SPY SYSTEM
The New Yorker, March 2, 1946.
The Wild Flag. Boston: Houghton Mifflin Co., 1946.

(THE IMPORTANCE OF) MANY NEWSPAPER OWNERS
The New Yorker, November 16, 1946.

LOVE AMONG THE FOREIGN OFFICES
The New Yorker, February 1, 1947.

DWINDLING OWNERSHIP OF THE PRESS
Letters of E. B. White, Revised Edition. Ed. Martha White.
　　New York: HarperCollins, 2006.

HERALD TRIBUNE ("HOLLYWOOD TEN" LETTERS)
Letters of E. B. White, Revised Edition. Ed. Martha White,
　　New York: HarperCollins, 2006.

LOYALTY
The New Yorker, December 6, 1947.

I SPY
The New Yorker, December 18, 1948.
Poems and Sketches of E. B. White. New York: Harper and
　　Row, 1981.

TEMPLE OF DEMOCRACY
The New Yorker, February 26, 1949.

DEATH OF THE *SUN*
The New Yorker, January 14, 1950.

THE THUD OF IDEAS
The New Yorker, September 23, 1950.
Writings from The New Yorker, *1925–1976*. Ed. Rebecca M.
　　Dale. New York: HarperCollins, 1990.

NOT CONFORMING TO FACTS
The New Yorker, December 9, 1950.

MURDER OF *LA PRENSA*
The New Yorker, March 31, 1951.

DISCREDIT OF OTHERS
The New Yorker, October 4, 1952.

THE ABC OF SECURITY
The New Yorker, May 9, 1953.

FCC BACKGROUND NOISE
The New Yorker, January 30, 1954.

ONE HOUR TO THINK
The New Yorker, May 22, 1954.

BEDFELLOWS
"A Letter from the East." February 6, 1956. Published in *The New Yorker*, February 18, 1956.
The Points of My Compass (with "P.S." from June 1962 added). New York: Harper and Row, 1962.
An E. B. White Reader. Ed. William W. Watt and Robert W. Bradford. New York: Harper and Row, 1966.
Essays of E. B. White. New York: Harper and Row, 1977
E. B. White on Dogs. Ed. Martha White. Thomaston, ME: Tilbury House Publishers, 2013.

KHRUSHCHEV AND I (A STUDY IN SIMILARITIES)
The New Yorker, September 26, 1959.
Writings from The New Yorker, *1925–1976*. Ed. Rebecca M. Dale. New York: HarperCollins, 1990.

UNITY
The New Yorker, June 18, 1960.
Congressional Record, June 29, 1960.
The Points of My Compass. New York: Harper and Row, 1962.
Essays of E. B. White. New York: Harper and Row, 1977.

BURDENS OF HIGH OFFICE
The New Yorker, October 12, 1963.

FREEDOM OF CHOICE
Weekly Packet, July 2, 1964.

DEMOCRACY IS DESTRUCTIBLE
Bangor Daily News, October 8, 1964.

MARGARET CHASE SMITH
Letters of E. B. White, Revised Edition. Ed. Martha White.
    New York: HarperCollins, 2006.

CARNEGIE COMMISSION ON EDUCATIONAL TELEVISION
Letter to Stephen White, September 26, 1966. In *Letters of
    E. B. White, Revised Edition.* Ed. Martha White. New
    York: HarperCollins, 2006.

PRESS MUST BE FREE
Bangor Daily News, November 5, 1970.

ON HOPE
Letter to Mr. Nadeau, March 30, 1973. *Letters of E. B. White,
    Revised Edition.* Ed. Martha White. New York: Harper-
    Collins, 2006.

DON'T BET ON IT
Bangor Daily News, March 27, 1975.

THE XEROX LETTERS
Ellsworth American, January 1, 1976.
Letters of E. B. White, Revised Edition. Ed. Martha White.
New York: HarperCollins, 2006.

REVERSES OF FORTUNE
The New Yorker, July 5, 1976.
"A Busy Place." *Writings from* The New Yorker, *1925–1976*.
Ed. Rebecca M. Dale. New York: HarperCollins, 1990.

Index

About the Author

E. B. WHITE (1899–1985), essayist, poet, humorist, and author, began his career as a contributor to *The New Yorker* in 1925, joining the staff in 1927. Over the years, he wrote more than twenty books, including the children's classics *Stuart Little*, *Charlotte's Web*, and *The Trumpet of the Swan*. He lived in New York City and Maine.

MARTHA WHITE, his granddaughter, lives on the coast of Maine.